# Leaking Laffs Between PAMPERS and DEPENDS

# Other Books by Barbara Johnson

*Where Does a Mother Go to Resign?*

*Fresh Elastic for Stretched-Out Moms*

*Stick a Geranium in Your Hat and Be Happy!*

*Splashes of Joy in the Cesspools of Life*

*Pack Up Your Gloomees in a Great Big Box,
Then Sit on the Lid and Laugh!*

*Mama, Get the Hammer! There's a Fly on Papa's Head!*

*I'm So Glad You Told Me What I Didn't Wanna Hear*

*Living Somewhere Between Estrogen and Death*

*Boomerang Joy*

*He's Gonna Toot, and I'm Gonna Scoot!*

## Children's Books

*The Upside-Down Frown and Splashes of Joy*

*Super-Scrumptious Jelly Donuts Sprinkled with Hugs*

*The Tasty Taffy Tale and Super-Stretching the Truth*

*The Pepperoni Parade and the Power of Prayer*

# BARBARA JOHNSON

## Leaking Laffs Between PAMPERS and DEPENDS

**WORD PUBLISHING**

NASHVILLE

A Thomas Nelson Company

Unless otherwise indicated, Scripture quotations used in this book are from the Holy Bible, New International Version (NIV). Copyright © 1973, 1978, 1984 International Bible Society. Used by permission of Zondervan Bible Publishers. Other Scripture references are from the following sources:

> The Holy Bible, New Century Version (NCV), copyright © 1987, 1988, 1991 by Word Publishing, Nashville, Tennessee. Used by permission.

> The King James Version of the Bible (KJV).

> The Living Bible (TLB). Copyright © 1971 by Tyndale House Publishers, Wheaton, Ill. Used by permission.

> *The Message* © 1994 by Eugene Patterson and published by NavPress, Colorado Springs, CO 80935. Used by permission.

Jokes, stories, and quips included in this volume have been contributed by the author's many friends, and we have diligently tried to identify the material's origin. Where no source is named, the writer is unknown, and the author disclaims any ownership or control of rights to this unattributed material. Please contact the publisher if you can positively identify the source of any unattributed jokes or stories, and proper attribution will be made in future printings.

**Library of Congress Cataloging-in-Publication Data**

Johnson, Barbara (Barbara E.)
   Leaking laffs between Pampers and Depends / by Barbara Johnson.
      p.   cm.
   ISBN 0-8499-3705-1 (trade paper)
   1. Motherhood. 2. Motherhood—Humor. 3. Parenting. 4. Parenting—Humor. I. Title.
HQ759.J6199   2000
306.874'3—dc21

00-020796
CIP

*Printed in the United States of America.*
00 01 02 03 04 05 06 QPV 9 8 7 6 5 4 3 2 1

*What a delight for me to dedicate this book to*
*Larrene Hagaman,*
*whose clever idea adorns*
*the cover and whose bubbly personality*
*and infectious enthusiasm*
*have made her my*
*favorite co-conspirator in*
*Leaking Laffs*
*wherever we go!*

# CONTENTS

*You shall be called the repairer of the breach. . . .*
—ISAIAH 58:12 NRSV

# Having a Baby Is Like Writing a Book—Lots of Whining, Begging, and Pushing

## *Chaos, Panic, and Disorder— My Work Here Is Done*

Someone commented recently that having a baby is a lot like writing a book.[1] As a woman who has given birth to four sons and written more than a dozen books, I should know!

The baby often begins as a spark—a little twinkle in someone's eye. The same thing happens when a book is conceived—a little spark in the brain sends emotions soaring in anticipation. No doubt about it: *Conceiving* a baby—or a book—is the easiest part of the whole project!

From that tiny seed, a baby is formed inside the mother's body. In the author's mind, an idea develops into the framework of the book; a few choice thoughts slowly grow into a chapter-by-chapter outline. At this stage, we parents-to-be start having daydreams filled with precious cherubs and darling little bundles of joy snoozing sweetly in nurseries decorated by Martha Stewart. Expectant authors imagine a spellbinding book that outsells everything but the Bible.

1

Then the pregnancy is confirmed. A contract is signed, and a due date is given. (*How could anything so wonderful have an awful name like "deadline"?* I wonder.) The date seems so far off . . . a few seasons or perhaps almost a whole year away. Actually the date may seem like a cloud of fog far in the distant future. There's so much time—no need to rush things. Like Scarlett O'Hara, I push any worries aside while pulling the dessert plate closer or filling the schedule a little fuller— and trilling "fiddle-dee-dee!" all the while.

Next comes that queasy feeling in the stomach, a nauseous reminder each morning that I've made a real, almost overwhelming commitment. Suddenly I feel an urge to upchuck before breakfast, after meals, or anytime I happen to walk by the typewriter that waits, cold and silent, on the desk in my bedroom. The idea of becoming a parent suddenly takes on a more serious tone. The bare framework of the book has formed, but there's precious little hanging on it.

Then comes the stage when I feel a deep desire that this pregnancy had not happened. There are even occasional feelings of resentment toward my husband (or my publisher). Is this person intentionally trying to annoy me? Why else am I

constantly bombarded with pesky reminders and nervous questions about what I'm eating or how much I've written? And why, in the quiet darkness at midnight, do I seem to hear a clock ticking somewhere or the pages of a calendar being flipped?

Then the second three months begin, and gradually I warm to the idea again. It actually starts to seem possible that I *can* be a mother, that I *can* write a book . . . but now the IBM Selectric seems too close to my swelling abdomen and too far from my outstretched fingertips. A mysterious restlessness fills my days as I wrestle with the ideas—and the individual—churning inside of me.

Now the baby seems to intrude on everything I do, and it's not even born yet. At this stage, going out to lunch means not just squeezing my bulky form behind a tiny table at a favorite restaurant but also asking to be seated on the outside to allow room for that huge lump in front of me. It seems to be the center of attention everywhere I go. Folks who hardly know me feel free to pat my tummy or put a sympathetic arm around my shoulders and ask how far along I am. Everything centers around the baby—or the book—that is not nearly finished yet.

**"That better not be my birthday present!"**

As the third trimester begins, I am exhausted and sick of seeing myself in mirrors, tired of feeling so bulky. I try to type out the words, but some strange interference causes me to have to strain to get at the typewriter. Everything seems to be moving farther away from my immense middle, my book-filled brain. What an effort it takes to do anything!

The last month is the worst. I know the baby is just about due. The book is almost finished, but at this point I don't care about the ending—or the beginning or middle, for that matter. I am so sorry I ever even thought of getting pregnant, regretful that I ever had the idea of writing a book. Then the baby is born. With deep groans of agony and heaving sighs of pain, I force out the last few pages, thinking, *I JUST WANT THIS TO BE OVER!* With my last ounce of strength, I lug the manuscript to the post office and mail it off to the publisher. Returning home and collapsing into bed, I heave a huge sigh of relief when the delivery is complete.

Then there is that brief, eager time after the birth when I hold my breath and wait for the doctor's (or the publisher's) assessment—to which I respond, "What do you mean the color seems to be a little off?" "How could you possibly think this masterpiece is too lengthy?" What follows next is sometimes the most irritating part of the whole process as my book is probed and preened until I beg for mercy. I threaten to take my poor baby and move to the home for the bewildered.

Then the nurses place my sweet angel on the pillow next to me. The editors show me the cleaned-up version, and glory be! It's kinda cute. A few weeks later, it's introduced around the neighborhood—or the world—and what do you know? People ogle it and . . . why, they actually like it! Trying to be modest, I blush and smile while proudly claiming it as my own.

Then, basking in the glow of adoration and appreciation, the most amazing miracle of all happens. Somewhere inside my head, all the memories of my recent agony melt away, and there's a tiny flash of brilliant light, one bright little spark.

And somehow I have the thought that . . . well, actually, it might be nice to have another one . . .

**THE FAMILY CIRCUS.**    By Bil Keane

"It's better than audio books, TV or
the Internet. It's called reading."

That's exactly how this book came about. After "giving
birth" to the book *Living Somewhere Between Estrogen and Death,*
I was so relieved to have it finished that I actually thought of
unplugging my IBM Selectric and calling it quits. After all,
I'm well into retirement age, and we "mature" mothers and
authors do need our rest. (By the way, you know why women
over fifty don't have babies, don't you? We'd put 'em down
somewhere and forget where we left them!)

After my *Estrogen* "baby" left home and went out into the
marketplace, I was inundated with stories and letters from
women who wanted to share their own hilarious "wonders of
womanhood." They also wanted to tell me how the book had
helped them laugh while they wrestled with the most heartbreaking experiences life could throw at them. One of my
favorite stories came from a woman who said she had read
the book aloud to her elderly mother as the loved one died of
cancer. "Barb, the nurses kept coming into the room and asking what was going on. You see, they weren't used to hearing
such laughter in the hospice center," she said.

That story warmed my heart! And so did a similar story shared by a woman in Chicago. She and her sister had brought along a copy of *Estrogen* when their eighty-year-old mother was hospitalized for what they feared was her final illness. Sitting in their mother's hospital room, they took turns reading the book aloud to her. She said, "Barb, I'll always be grateful to you for that cherished image: my mother, *laughing,* on her deathbed!"

"Oh," I answered softly, "when did she die?"

"Oh, she didn't die—she lived!" the woman said, laughing heartily. "That was a year ago. She's fine now. We think it was all that *Estrogen* we read to her and all that laughing!"

Another woman came to my book table at a conference and told me she had first seen *Estrogen* when she was sharing a reception area with other women awaiting radiation treatment for cancer. One of the women, she said, was reading the book and chuckling to herself. Seeing the expectant faces of the other women waiting with her, she began to read aloud. Pretty soon, the woman said as she tugged on the geranium-trimmed hat covering her bald head, "We were all roaring with laughter."

Such responses helped make *Estrogen* the number one best-selling paperback book for the whole Christian market in 1997, the year it was published![2] When the standings were announced, I thought, *This must be how it feels to be the mother of Miss America!* With the encouragement of so many readers and with an abundance of delightful new material flowing in, everyone agreed there had to be another book. But while *Estrogen* was aimed at women living somewhere "between menopause and LARGE PRINT," the material that had been shared by all the letter-writers and Women of Faith conference attendees clearly indicated that the next book would need to encompass *all* the years of a woman's life, ranging from parenting young children to parenting parents. The first seed for the title came from a gal at a Women of Faith conference somewhere who laughingly told me she was "somewhere between Pampers and Depends."

## Naming the Baby

Parents know how important it is to choose the perfect name for their baby. You have to consider what words rhyme with the name so you don't choose something the poor kid can be tortured with by his or her peers. It's nice to choose a biblical name—while keeping modern trends in mind. David and Benjamin are very popular, for example, but Damaris and Boaz are less common these days. The best names bring to mind a positive image of a happy, trustworthy person.

The same is true for book titles. Authors and publishers go round and round trying to choose a name that will accurately represent the book while igniting a spark in the minds of potential readers. One of my all-time favorite book titlers is Dave Barry. A few years ago he published a book titled *Babies and Other Hazards of Sex*. Frankly, the *title* wasn't all that great, but the *subtitle* was hilarious: *How to Make a Tiny Person in Nine Months with Tools You Probably Have Around the House.*

Hoping for a phrase as clever as that one, I suggested to my publisher that the phrase "Pampers and Depends" was the heart of a great book title. At first, the Word Publishing executives were okay with it. One Word executive even sent me a fax, excitedly sharing that she'd found the word *pampers* in her Bible concordance: "Of course, it's not the diaper kind," she wrote, "but I thought it was funny to see it there. The reference is Proverbs 29:21: "If a man pampers his servant from youth, he will bring grief in the end."

Not being a real pious prune, I took that as a sign that God was bestowing His blessing on our next project, even if the context didn't seem to be related in any way. So we had part of a title, but we needed a verb. We'd already used *living*, so something different was needed. Someone suggested *changing*, citing all the changes we women go through—changing diapers, changing from daughters to mothers to grandmothers, going through the *change.*

But *changing* seemed so ordinary. In the middle of the night (it might have been a rainy night), the word *leaking* suddenly

**What mothers think of when someone
suggests they can change the world.**

soaked into my brain. It felt like a logical choice to me. But the
poor folks at Word nearly croaked when I mentioned it!

"Oh, Barb, you don't mean it!" one of them gasped.
"*Leaking* diapers?"

"Barb, that's just too gross," another one moaned. (It might
have been the same one who worried a few years ago that the
Christian market just wasn't ready for the word *cesspools* in my
best-selling book titled *Splashes of Joy in the Cesspools of Life.*)

"Well," I reminded them self-righteously, "you just need to
remember Philippians 4:8 and think on things that are pure
and lovely. Obviously, you've got *your* minds somewhere
else!" (Because I've been working with these dear people for
nearly a decade, I tend to offer them a little motherly advice
and scriptural insights now and then.)

As we continued "negotiating," I sent out a short list of title
options to a couple hundred friends and supporters of
Spatula Ministries, asking their opinions. The overwhelming
response from these women was that *leaking laffs* was the best
possible choice. As one woman wrote, "The word *changing* is
boring. *Leaking* is best!"

Meanwhile, back in Nashville, the Word executives were

probably pulling their hair out and stocking up on extra-strength Maalox.

After several weeks of whining and begging (I whined, they begged), I had just about persuaded them to let me have my way when something happened that settled the issue once and for all. To express our appreciation for the artwork Precious Moments creator Sam Butcher had generously donated to my last book, *He's Gonna Toot and I'm Gonna Scoot*, Word had graciously prepared a beautifully poignant plaque to give him. The presentation was made at the Women of Faith conference in Kansas City, after which some of my favorite Word executives whisked us off to lunch at a cozy restaurant where we had a special room all to ourselves.

During lunch, I waited for a quiet moment, then, with the Word people listening, I casually asked Sam for his opinion on the title I was proposing for my next book. The picture below shows Sam's merry response. He burst out laughing, rocking back and forth in his chair, and then added between guffaws, "And you could have babies in diapers crawling along the bottom of the cover and call them 'little squirts'!"

*My delightful friend Sam Butcher, creator of Precious Moments, loved the title I proposed for this book.*

Of course, this just about sent the frazzled Word folks over the edge. Judging by the stiff smiles that seemed to be frozen on their sweet faces, I thought they all might be considering a career change at precisely that moment. But when they could speak again they swallowed hard and graciously nodded their assent (probably while wondering if their therapists offered telephone counseling on Saturday).

The "baby" had been named!

Later, Sam's sharp-witted assistant, Larrene Hagaman, pulled the whole idea together by suggesting the cover illustration: the Geranium Lady riding a waterspout that's shooting up through a small boat. At one end of the boat, Sam's "little squirt" is yowling away, and at the other end there's Larrene's "little squint" (who looks a little like Mammy Yokum), enjoying the ride. When Word's artist, Dennis Hill, sent me his depiction of these little characters, I knew they were too adorable to use just once. So you'll find them popping up again in the collections of jokes and stories that close out each chapter. In fact, I've called these chapter-closing giggles "Squirts & Squints," just because the whole idea makes me laugh!

## Toot 'n' What?

Even when I have to work hard at negotiating (begging and whining) to get the book titles I want for my "babies," I enjoy every minute of it. All the whining just makes for a better story in the end, which I love to share with folks who ask, "Where in the world did you get that title?"

It's also fun to see how the titles get mangled and twisted. For example, after *Toot 'n' Scoot* was published last year, I got an early morning call from a lady in West Virginia who said, "I heard on the radio that you have a new book out, and I wanted to read it. But it's forty miles to the nearest Christian bookstore, so I want to make sure I get the right one. It sounded like you said the title is *Poop 'n' Scoop*. Could that be right?" And at my book table somewhere, a woman said she thought the title was called *Too Pooped to Scoot!*

Another woman sent a note to my publisher that said:

Barbara Johnson will love this . . . I sent my husband to the Christian bookstore to see if they had her new book, *He's Gonna Toot and I'm Gonna Scoot.* He proceeded to go in and ask for *One More Toot and I'm Gonna Move!* (I laughed 'til I cried!)

See what fun I'd miss if I didn't insist on giving my books such zany titles? Of course, I do get a little nervous when I think of the books' foreign translations, especially after reading the long list of nightmares someone sent to me that resulted when American companies' trade names were translated overseas. One of the marketing failures supposedly occurred when a company marketed a ballpoint pen in Mexico, where its ads were supposed to say, "It won't leak in your pocket and embarrass you." Instead, due to a faulty translation, the ads said, "It won't leak in your pocket and make you pregnant"!

**Leaking Laffs, Soaking Up Love**
Now, isn't this just like a new mother—spilling all the gory details of labor while visitors cuddle the baby? If you're a woman, I don't think you'll mind. In fact, you may want to send

**HERMAN**®

3-11    © Jim Unger/dist. by United Media, 1999

**"Can't you ever get sick without bringing home one of th_e?"**

me your own "triumphant" stories of childbirth and parenting experiences—whatever you've birthed and experienced!

And if you're a man—well, buddy, hang on to your hairpiece! If you're gonna read *this* book, you'd better prepare yourself for some mental aerobics. And your eyebrows may get a workout, too, if they're not used to frequent lifting. Don't be embarrassed; I've learned to expect some men to let their curiosity get the better of them and read my books, even when they're warned not to. After we put a "For Women Only" disclaimer on the cover of *Estrogen*, I heard from one man who joked that he'd read it by flashlight while hiding in the closet. Another man said he had propped it open in front of a newsmagazine so fellow airplane passengers wouldn't give him a hard time as he read. What a delightful picture those men must have made!

Like that famous deodorant line, this book is "strong enough for a man—but made for a woman." Whoever you are, and wherever you are along the journey from Pampers to Depends, I hope you'll come along to share some "laff leaks" in this boatload of silliness. We're gonna have a fabulous time, splashing in laughter and soaking up God's love.

"...THE ONLY REAL PROBLEM IS I KEEP GETTING HIS 'PAMPERS' MIXED UP WITH MY 'DEPENDS'..."

62 YR. OLD WOMAN HAS BABY

Unless otherwise indicated, the sources of all the "squirts and squints" in this book are unknown; people who know how much I love to laugh have sent me these little ditties in letters or faxes or passed them to me on scraps of paper at Women of Faith conferences. I'm grateful to these unnamed writers, whoever they are. Their words have touched my heart—and tickled my funny bone.

# Squirts & Squints

I love deadlines.

I especially like the *whooshing* sound they make as they go flying by!

A little boy told his preschool teacher one morning, "I have a disappointment I want to talk about in circle time."

"Ohhhh," said his teacher, worried he might be planning to spill some devastating family news. "Could you tell me first?"

"No," he replied solemnly. "I want to tell everyone."

She tried to persuade him to give her a preview of his "disappointment," but he stubbornly refused to say another word until his little classmates were assembled in the sharing-time circle.

Nervously, the teacher waited. When it was his turn, the little boy took a breath and started telling about lying down on a big chair that lifted him up toward a bright light. A man wearing a mask told him to open his mouth and then tapped on his teeth with something hard, he said.

It was then that the preschool teacher realized just what the little tike was describing: his *dentist appointment*.

—JULIE HENDRY

Think it over. Of all the creatures God created, we are the only ones that have to deal with diapers. Consider the lilies of the field; they neither toil nor spin nor clean up after their junior lily offspring. . . . [Perhaps] God deliberately chose to create our babies as hygienically challenged little people who require our extremely personal service several times each day . . . to ensure that we learn to perform a selfless act on behalf of a truly helpless person who cannot even thank us, doesn't really know what we are doing for him anyway, and, more likely than not, will [wet] on us for good measure. . . .

Changing the baby is sort of like giving alms in secret, only smellier.[3]

Some time ago, a tiny three-year-old daughter used a whole roll of gold wrapping paper to wrap a present for her father. Money was tight for the family, and when the little girl brought the gift to him, her father winced to see how much of the expensive paper had been used. Then his anger flared when he found that the box, so elaborately wrapped, was completely empty.

"Don't you know that when you give someone a present, there's supposed to be something inside of it?" he snapped. "You've wasted all this paper on an empty box."

The little girl looked up at him with tears in her eyes and said, "Oh, Daddy! It's not empty. I blew kisses into the box. They're for you, Daddy."

Each of us parents has been given a gold box filled with unconditional love from our children. There is no more precious possession anyone could hold.

When it's hard to go with the flow . . .
at least try to trickle!

—Patprints Calendar

You know you're a mother when . . .

- You have time to shave only one leg at a time.
- You've mastered the art of placing large quantities of different foods on a plate without anything touching.
- You hear your own mother's voice coming out of your mouth.
- You use your own saliva to clean your child's face.

The boss urgently needed to speak to one of his employees on a Saturday afternoon. He dialed the employee's home number and was greeted with a child's whispered, "Hello?"

"Is your daddy home?" the boss asked.

"Yes," whispered the small voice.

"May I speak to him?" the boss queried.

"No," the little kid answered.

His patience running thin, the boss asked next, "Well, is your mommy there?"

"Yes," came the whispered reply.

"May I speak to her?"

Again the small voice whispered, "No."

Perplexed, the boss asked, "Well are there any other adults there?"

"Yes," the child whispered, "a policeman."

Stunned, the boss hesitated only a moment and then asked, "Well, may I speak with the policeman?"

"No, he's busy," whispered the child.

"Busy doing what?" the boss asked.

"Talking to Daddy and Mommy and the fireman," the child replied.

"There's a policeman and a fireman there?" the boss said, now beginning to get worried. "Why are they there?"

Still whispering, the young voice replied with a muffled giggle, "They're looking for *me!*"

When my friend Roger Shouse wrote to wish me "best of luck with the new book," he struggled to find the right phrase. "With actors they say, 'Break a leg.' But what do they tell authors? 'Get a cramp in the hand?' 'Hope your mind goes blank'?"

A little girl was diligently pounding away on her father's computer. She told him she was writing a story. "What's it about?" he asked.

"I don't know," she replied. "I can't read."

A grandmother wasn't sure her granddaughter had learned her colors yet, so she decided to test her. She repeatedly pointed out things and asked the tiny girl what color it was. The girl always answered correctly. But it was fun for the grandma, so she continued the game. Finally the little grand-daughter headed for the door, saying sagely, "Grandma, I think you should try to figure out some of these yourself!"

The only time a woman wishes she were a year older is
when she is expecting a baby.

A woman took her small daughter to the funeral home for the viewing of her great-grandmother. Staring, perplexed, into the casket, the little girl asked, "Mama, why did they put Great-grandma in a jewelry box?"

Someone has equated laughter with changing a baby's diaper: "It doesn't change things permanently, but it makes every-thing OK for a while."

A couple invited some people to dinner. At the table, the father asked their six-year-old daughter to say the blessing.

"I don't know what to say," the girl replied.

"Just say what you hear Mommy say," the dad answered.

The daughter bowed her head, heaved a little sigh, and said, "Lord, why on earth did we invite all these people to dinner?"

An old country doctor went way out into the boonies to deliver a baby. It was so far out, there was no electricity. When the doctor arrived, no one was home except for the laboring mother and her five-year-old son. The doctor instructed the child to hold a lantern high so he could see to deliver the baby. The child held the lantern, the mother pushed, and after a little while, the doctor lifted the newborn baby by the feet and swatted him on the bottom to get him to take his first breath.

Watching in wide-eyed wonder, the five-year-old shouted, "Hit him again! He shouldn't have crawled up there in the first place!"

Little kids' instructions on life:

- When your dad is mad and asks you, "Do I look stupid?" don't answer him.
- Never try to baptize a cat.
- Never trust a dog to watch your food.
- Never tell your little brother that you're not going to do what your mom told you to do.
- Remember you're never too old to hold your father's hand.

I went to a bookstore and asked the saleswoman, "Where's the self-help section?"

She said if she told me, it would defeat the purpose.

—STEVEN WRIGHT

A mom was delivering a station wagon full of kids home from nursery school one day when a fire truck zoomed past. Sitting in the front seat beside the driver was a Dalmatian dog. The children began discussing the dog's duties.

"They use him to keep crowds back," said one youngster.

"No," said another, "he's just for good luck."

A third child brought the argument to a close. "They use the dog," she said firmly, "to find the fire hydrant."

A couple of young siblings were sitting together in church. Finally, the six-year-old sister had had enough of her little brother's giggling and talking out loud. "You're not supposed to talk out loud in church," she hissed at him.

"Why? Who's going to stop me?" the little boy challenged.

The big sister pointed to the back of the church and said, "See those two men standing by the door? They're *hushers*."

A mother was preparing pancakes for her sons, Kevin, five, and Ryan, three. The boys began to argue over who would get the first pancake. Their mother saw the opportunity for a moral lesson. "If Jesus were sitting here, He would say, 'Let my brother have the first pancake. I can wait.'"

There was a pause, and then Kevin turned to his younger brother and said, "Ryan, you be Jesus."[4]

"God has made me laugh. Everyone who hears about this will laugh with me."

—SARAH, AGED WIFE OF ONE-
HUNDRED-YEAR-OLD ABRAHAM,
UPON THE BIRTH OF THEIR SON,
ISAAC (GEN. 21:6 NCV)

# Who Are These Kids, and Why Are They Calling Me Mom?

## Babies and Other Terrorists . . .

The Women of Faith conference rolled into Kansas City over Mother's Day weekend last year, and we opened the newspaper that Sunday morning to find a colorful article featuring profiles of the area's wackiest moms: "a motherlode of moms who keep their kids in stitches," the headline proclaimed. Reading the profiles, I felt a strong bond with these zany mamas. Even though I'd never met any of them, I had a feeling it would be fun to get together with them and trade comedy secrets.

For example, there was this story one daughter told about her laughter-loving mother: "Many years ago, my mother was in the kitchen fixing dinner, washing this raw chicken. My sister and I walked in, and she stuck her hand inside the chicken, like a puppet, and she pulled up a wing and said, 'Wave to the girls! Wave to Jane! Wave to Ellen!' And she's dancing around with this chicken. We stood there with our mouths hanging open. Now we almost can't eat chicken—it's like eating a friend."

Another girl tattled that her mother cleaned house wearing

"pink and red tutus." When the kids misbehaved, the daughter said, this mom took mug shots of them and then fingerprinted them as though she were booking them for the lockup.

As a gift for another mom's seventieth birthday her children "made up a booklet of all the goofy, weird things she's done over the years—she's pulled some real lulus." One incident described when she took her car to the mechanic because the motor was racing. That was back when cars had a manual choke knob on the dashboard. "She had pulled the choke out a foot and a half and was using it to hang her purse on," her adult son wrote fondly.

The newspaper included several more accounts by children who had written the newspaper to describe the gift of laughter their mothers had given them.[1] One daughter wrote that she had learned from her mother, "With enough practice, joy becomes as natural as breathing, and such a habit that it just comes out of your body."[2]

Reading those stories, I started to think maybe I wasn't such a weird parent after all. So what if I had joined my boys all those years ago in flicking red Jell-O on the white kitchen wall? And maybe I wasn't so odd in tricking my son Steve into thinking I'd accidentally boiled his favorite green wool sweater (I left a cute little doll's sweater, exactly the same color, in its place in his drawer).

A mother's love is one of the most important things a child can ever know. But there's another gift that enriches a child's life beyond measure. Blessed indeed are the children whose memories are filled with the familiar sound of their mother's laughter entwined with their own.

### The Evolution of a Mom
As you might guess, I love to laugh. It's been one of the strongest fibers in the lifeline God has used to pull me from a variety of heartbreaking pits—my husband's devastating accident, the deaths of two sons, and the eleven-year alienation of another. If I hadn't been able to find some laughter in all these

ordeals, I'd surely be making potholders today in a mental ward or bouncing around in a padded cell somewhere!

Instead, I'm blessed with a very active speaking career, in addition to my work with Spatula Ministries. As you read in Chapter 1, my "babies" these days are made of paper and ink instead of flesh and blood, but there are still a lot of similarities between becoming an author and becoming a parent. And no matter what you title *your* baby, you'll surely agree that the process of becoming a parent changes everything.

Indeed, there is an evolution to becoming a mother that is an ever-ongoing thing. Recently I saw another book that emphasized this point. It was entitled *So You Thought You Were Done with It!* and it exemplified that parenthood is never over. As I like to say, once you become a mother it's like getting a life sentence in prison with no hope of parole! And no matter how old we get, we mothers watch our kids—even when they're middle-aged—for signs of improvement. We're always hoping that something we instilled in them MIGHT show up, even when we've started to think it's too late.

**Committed**

Yes, becoming a parent changes everything, but parenthood itself also changes with each baby. For example, consider your wardrobe. As soon as the pregnancy home test kit confirms that you're pregnant, you head for the mall—and come home wearing a maternity outfit. With the second baby, you squeeze into your regular clothes as long as possible.

With the third baby, your maternity clothes ARE your regular clothes!

Then there's your preparation for labor and delivery. With the first baby you attend weekly classes and faithfully practice your breathing. With the second baby, you try to keep breathing when you find your two-year-old teetering at the top of the basement stairs.

With the third baby, you threaten to hold your breath indefinitely unless the doctor gives you an epidural in your second trimester!

Collecting the first baby's layette is always fun. You spend hours shopping for just the right curtains, blankets, and crib ruffle and the carefully prewash the tiny little gowns and booties with Woolite. For the second baby, you adjust the curtains and ruffles so the projectile-vomiting stains don't show and bleach everything else in hot water to disinfect it.

With the third child . . . you move to Florida so the baby needs no clothes at all—just disposable diapers.

A new baby can cause overwhelming fatigue, so parents adapt different stress-coping strategies with each child. For instance, with the first baby, you worry so much about the baby's cries that you never put the infant down—you wear her constantly in a baby carrier strapped to your chest. When the second baby cries, you pick him up only when his hysterics threaten to wake up your firstborn.

With the third child, you teach your other two kids where to look for the pacifier and how to rewind the baby swing.

Parents' dealings with baby-sitters also change. The first time you leave your baby with a sitter, you conduct a two-hour training session for the caregiver, then call home four times while you run to the post office. With the second baby, just before you walk out the door you remember to leave an emergency phone number—your neighbor's.

With the third baby, you tell the sitter to call only if someone needs stitches, splints, or an ambulance.

Baby activities change too. You take your first infant to baby swim classes, baby aerobics, and baby massage. You take your second baby to baby story hour so you can nap while the story is read.

You take the third baby to the McDonald's drive-through.

You use your time differently as each child comes along. You spend hours each day staring adoringly at your precious first infant. With the second baby, you glance in her direction occasionally as you race to stop your toddler from dropping the cat down the laundry chute.

With the third child, you train the dog to guard the baby from his siblings a few hours each day while you hide in the closet.

While I love to laugh *now* at such silly evolutions, I do remember that babies can be fabulous—and lots of fun. A baby is a small member of the family who can make the love stronger, the days shorter, the nights longer, and the bankroll

© 1999. Reprinted courtesy of Bunny Hoest and *Parade* magazine.

**"Your father and I have *always* wanted more children.
It's not a reflection on your performance."**

smaller. When a baby is born, the home will be happier—even if the clothes are shabbier. The past is forgotten, and the future is worth living for. And when *more* babies come along, the work is multiplied, that's true; but so are the joy and the love.

We mothers of multiple children like to say we love all our kids equally, but in our heart of hearts, we know that's not true. It's like the mother of several children answered when a reporter asked her, "Which of your children do you love the most?"

The wise and loving mother replied, "I love the one most who is away from home until he returns; the one who is sick until he is well; the one who is hurt until the hurt disappears; and the one who is lost until he is found."[3]

### Moms and Angels

Once children come along, a woman's identity is changed irrevocably. There's no feeling on earth like the twist of the

**THE FAMILY CIRCUS.**        **By Bil Keane**

Reprinted with permission of Bil Keane.

"I know why the car pool's so late, Mommy! This
is OUR morning to drive!"

heart at that moment when a tiny youngster links that syllable, *Ma,* with the face of its mother. A connection is formed, and whether it evolves into the name Mom or Mama or Mother, it is a name that is as common as breath itself—and as unique as each set of two hearts it links.

Someone sent me a beautiful bookmark that says, "On the day we are born, God gives each of us a beautiful guardian angel: and as we grow, we give her a name . . . Mother."

Then there's this beautiful little essay:

### The Angel

Up in heaven a child was ready to be born. The child asked God, "I know You are sending me to earth tomorrow, but how can I survive there? I am so small and helpless."

God replied, "I have chosen a special angel for you there. She will love you and take care of you."

"Here in heaven, Lord, I don't do anything but sing and smile. What will I do on Earth? I won't know how to sing the songs down there."

"Your angel will sing for you," God replied, "and she'll teach you how to sing, too. And you'll learn to laugh as well as smile. Your angel and I will take care of that."

"But how will I understand what people say to me? I don't know a single word of the language they speak!"

"Your angel will say the sweetest things you will ever hear, and she will teach you, word by word, how to speak the language."

"And when I want to talk to You . . . ?"

"Your angel will gently place your little hands together and teach you how. That's the simplest language of all. It's called prayer."

"Who will protect me there, God?"

"Your angel is soft and gentle, but if something threatens you, there is no stronger force on Earth than the power she'll use to defend you."

"I'll be sad not getting to see You anymore."

"I will always be next to you, even though you can't see Me. And your angel will teach you the way to come back to Me if you stray."

Then it was time to go. Excited voices could be heard from earth, anticipating the child's arrival. In a hurry, the babe asked softly, "Oh, God, if I must go now, please tell me my angel's name!"

And God replied, "You will call your angel . . . *Mommy.*"

—Source Unknown

**Are You Ready for Motherhood?**

Now, if you're wondering whether you have what it takes to be a *mommy,* here's a list of preparations to help you get ready for the blessed event:

*Mother's Preparation for Pregnancy:* From the food co-op, obtain a twenty-five-pound bag of pinto beans and attach it to your waist with a belt. Wear it everywhere you go for nine months. Then remove ten of the beans to indicate the baby has been born.

*Financial Preparation:* Arrange for direct deposit of your family's paycheck to be split equally between the nearest grocery store and the pediatrician's office for the next two decades.

*Mess-Management Preparation:* Smear grape jelly on the living room furniture and curtains. Now plunge your hands into a bag of potting soil, wipe them on the walls, and highlight the smudges with Magic Markers.

*Inhalation Therapy Preparation:* Empty a carton of milk onto the cloth upholstery of the family car, park the vehicle in a sunny spot, and then leave it to ripen for the month of August. Rub a half-finished lollipop through your hair, then hide it in the glove compartment.

*Pain-Endurance Preparation:* Collect enough small, plastic, superhero action figures to fill a fifty-five gallon drum.

(You may substitute thumbtacks.) Ask a friend to spread them all over the floor of your house after you've gone to bed, paying special attention to the stairway. Set your alarm for 2 A.M., and when it goes off, rush madly around the darkened house, trying to remember where you left the cordless phone (for the baby).

*Shopping Preparation:* Herd a flock of goats through the grocery store. Always keep every goat in sight and bring enough money to pay for whatever they eat or destroy.

*Aerobic-Agility Preparation:* Try to dress the family cat in a small pantsuit, complete with button shirt, snap-leg pants, lace-up shoes, and a bowtie while the neighbor's German shepherd barks out his encouragement from two feet away. (Make sure medics are standing by.)

*Mealtime Preparation:* Sit at the kitchen counter and carefully spoon strained peas and chocolate pudding into a plastic bag. When the bag is completely full, tie a knot to close it, place it on the kitchen counter at eye level about a foot from your face, then ask your spouse to smash the bag with a dictionary.

*Attitude Preparation:* Have a schoolteacher friend record the sounds of her second-graders scratching their fingernails across a chalkboard. Then fill a small canvas bag with ten pounds of cat litter, soak it thoroughly in water, attach the bag to a tape player with large speakers, and insert the nails-on-chalkboard recording. Beginning at 8 P.M., pick up the bag and hold it against your shoulder, play the chalkboard recording at its loudest volume, and waltz around the room with a bumping-and-swooping step. Continue for forty minutes, then gently lay down the bag and turn off the tape player. Repeat hourly until 5 A.M. Then crawl in bed, set the alarm for 6 A.M., get up and make breakfast while looking cheerful. Repeat for the next five years.

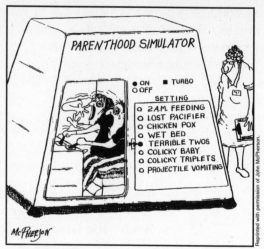

**In an effort to prepare expectant parents for the challenges that lie ahead, many obstetricians' offices have installed parenthood simulators.**

The funny thing about these silly preparations is that somehow all of us parents pass it when we have to. (Well, maybe not the part about looking cheerful while cooking breakfast, but the rest of it, we usually muddle through.) If you're in the middle of the "testing" period right now, remember that you're enrolled in a course that's been a perpetual requirement since Adam and Eve. You *will* get through it (unless, of course, you end up weaving doilies in the home for the bewildered first!). And *someday* you'll be rewarded. As actress Meryl Streep commented recently, "You don't really read the results of [your mothering efforts] until way late in life. Usually, it's the adult child who looks back and thinks: How did she do all of that? How did she stay in a good mood all the time? . . . If you're a mom, you know how much you're doing, but you're not going to get a lot of credit for it. Mothering is an invisible achievement."[4]

## Help from Above
Mothers need all the help they can get these days to achieve their overwhelming goal, even though a recent study showed

that "motherhood may actually make women smarter." The increased intellect is due to "hormones released during pregnancy and nursing [that] dramatically enrich parts of the brain involved in learning and memory."[5] When I saw that, I thought, *Wow! Just when we feel so exhausted we can hardly remember our own names, we're actually Einsteins in training!* How about that! Now if someone could just figure out how we could work on updating the theory of relativity while changing diapers, scraping *Star Wars* stickers off the car windows, and counting the sprinkles on cupcakes to make sure no one is shortchanged—we'd have it made!

No matter how smart we are, weary mothers need lots of help and encouragement—the kind that comes from family and friends, and especially the kind that comes from God. But sometimes we get so busy—and so exhausted—we forget to tap into this ultimate resource. Sometimes all it takes is a reminder. One friend of mine, the mother of two trying teenagers, bought herself a cheap digital watch that she set to softly chime every hour. "Throughout the day, whenever I heard that little beep," she said, "I paused a moment or two in whatever I was doing and whispered a little prayer on behalf of my kids."

She told her teenagers what she was doing, and the results were amazing. Her daughter, stressed out in her high school

**ZITS**

classroom and unable to focus on the test that lay on the desk before her, happened to look up at the clock. "It said ten o'clock, and I remembered that you were praying for me," she told her mother one day. "It was as if a very calming blanket of peace gently wrapped itself around me, and I was able to clear my head and finish the test." Her son confessed to similar results a few years later. "When I was a senior, there was one day when school was out for the day, and my buddies and I were out in the parking lot, talking about what we would do for the rest of the afternoon. They all decided that instead of going to their after-school jobs, they would hang out at the shopping mall awhile and see if there were any good-looking girls there. I was all set to go with them, but just then the bell in the church tower across the street chimed three o'clock, and I suddenly got an image of my mom, praying for me at that exact moment. I got in my car and went to work."

Last year many of us got a different kind of reminder to pray as we traveled city streets and interstate highways. The reminders were scattered all across the nation in the outdoor advertising industry's national public service campaign called "God Speaks." The messages appeared on ten thousand billboards throughout America, catching motorists' attention with their stark white letters on a solid black background. "We need to talk," one of them said. Like all the others, it was signed, "God."

The idea was started by a Florida resident who insisted on remaining anonymous but "wanted to reach people who used to go to church and for some reason don't go anymore," an advertising executive explained. Other messages in the campaign included:

- "C'mon over and bring the kids."

- "Will the road you're on get you to my place?"

- "Follow me."

- "Need directions?"

The one that touched my heart most tenderly was the one that said simply,

*Tell the kids I love them.*

—GOD[6]

Someone sent me a little prayer aid that's not only helpful for us parents to use but especially to teach to our children and grandchildren. It's a simple way to pray for others and ourselves by counting off the fingers of one hand. Its author is unknown, but I suspect she was a mother!

1. When you clasp your hands in prayer, your thumb is closest to you. So begin your prayer by remembering those closest to you—your children, parents, friends, and other loved ones.

2. The pointing finger is next. Pray for those who point the way for us: our teachers, ministers, mentors, and others who help us learn. Ask God to give them wisdom and courage to guide others in His truth and in His way.

3. The middle finger is the tallest one, reminding us to pray for our leaders in government, in business, and in our schools and churches. Ask God to help them heed His ways as they shape our nation and make decisions that affect all of us.

4. The ring finger is next. You might not realize it, but this finger, not the pinkie, is our weakest finger. Let it remind you to pray for those who are weak or sick or in trouble. Ask God to show them that they are weak but He is strong.

5. Then comes the smallest finger of all. This littlest finger reminds us that we are to put others before ourselves, even in prayer. By the time you have prayed for the needs of the other four groups of people—your loved ones, your teachers, your leaders, and those who

are sick and in trouble, your own needs will probably seem much less important. The little finger reminds us to pray for ourselves—and to hold to the Bible's promise that "the least shall be the greatest among you."

Whether you're reminded to pray by the beeping of a digital watch or by the sound of the phone ringing in the wee hours of the morning, if you're a mom you know prayer helps. One stage of parenting that generates *lots* of fervent prayers is surely the time when we're teaching our kids how to drive. Later—if we survive the high blood pressure and accelerated heart rates—the memories of these parent-and-teenager driving sessions can be funny, if not especially soothing. In my case, the memory of when I taught our son Tim to drive has become a cherished frozen picture in my mental scrapbook.

We went to a nearby cemetery so Tim could learn how to negotiate the narrow, curving roadway that wound through the grounds. It was the perfect place since the speed limit was about 15 and there usually weren't any other cars we could bump into. Still, there were a few screeches of the brakes and some wandering off the pavement occasionally. Now I laugh at those memories, and I'm so grateful for them when I go to that same cemetery . . . to visit Tim's grave.

**Murray's Law by Leslie Moak Murray**

It isn't easy being a mom, but prayer helps—and so does laughter. And sometimes it even helps to shed a cleansing tear or two. As someone said, tears are to the soul what soap is to the body. So let's end this chapter with both—jokes and tender stories about parenthood—squirts of tears and squints from the laughter.

## Squirts & Squints

**Bumper Sticker:**
If you can't laugh at yourself . . .
I'll be glad to do it for you.

If I had my child to raise all over again,
I'd finger paint more, and point the finger less.
I'd do less correcting, and more connecting.
I'd take my eyes off my watch, and watch with my eyes.
I would care to know less, and know to care more.
I'd take more hikes and fly more kites.
I'd stop playing serious, and seriously play.
I'd run through more fields, and gaze at more stars.
I'd do more hugging, and less tugging.
I would be firm less often, and affirm much more.
I'd build self-esteem first, and the house later.
I'd teach less about the love of power,
And more about the power of love.

—DIANE LOOMANS[7]

Things moms would probably never say:
—"How on earth can you see the TV sitting so far back?"
—"Yeah, I used to skip school a lot, too."

—"Just leave all the lights on . . . we have extra money this month for the bill."

—"Let me smell that shirt. Yeah, that's good for another week."

—"Go ahead and keep that stray dog, honey; I'll be glad to take care of it for you."

—"Well, if Timmy's mom says it's okay, that's good enough for me!"

—"The curfew is just a general time to shoot for—give or take three or four hours."

—"I don't have a tissue with me . . . just wipe your nose on your sleeve."

—"Don't bother wearing a jacket. The wind chill is bound to improve."[8]

The heart of a mother is a deep abyss at the bottom of which you will always discover forgiveness.

—HONORÉ DE BALZAC

A teacher asked her Sunday school class to draw pictures of their favorite Bible stories. She was puzzled by Jimmy's picture, which showed four people on an airplane. She asked him what story he meant.

"The flight to Egypt," Jimmy said.

"I see. And that must be Mary, Joseph, and Baby Jesus," the teacher answered. "But who's the fourth person?"

"Oh, that's Pontius—the pilot!"

More truths brought to us by children:

—Don't let your mom brush your hair when she's mad at your dad.

—If your sister hits you, don't hit her back. It's always the second person who gets caught.

—Dogs still have bad breath even after a squirt of breath freshener.

—Never hold the cat while the vacuum cleaner is running.

—When you're in trouble the best place to be is in Grandma's lap.

I note with great interest that when God made the first human being, Adam, He created him as a complete adult and thus totally bypassed diapers, colic, toddlerhood, adolescence, and driving lessons. . . .

My personal theory is that God designed parenthood, in part, as an enormous character-building exercise, and since God does not personally require character improvement, He didn't need to bother getting Adam to eat strained peas.[9]

After putting her children to bed, a mother changed into old slacks and a droopy blouse and then washed her hair in the sink and smeared her face with a slick, green moisturizing cream that hardened into a mask. As she heard the children getting more and more rambunctious, her patience evaporated. At last she threw a towel around her dripping hair and stormed into their room, threatening all sorts of dire punishments if they didn't get back into bed and go to sleep.

As she left the room, she heard a small voice whisper in the darkness, "Who *was* that?"

### THE FAMILY CIRCUS®          By Bil Keane

"I'm grounded. I said one more word
to my mother."

At the end of the school year, a kindergarten teacher was receiving gifts from her pupils. The florist's son handed her a gift. She shook it, held it overhead, and said, "I bet I know what it is: some flowers."

"That's right," the boy said, "but how did you know?"

"Oh, just a wild guess," she answered.

The next pupil was the sweet-shop owner's daughter. The teacher held her gift overhead, shook it, and said, "I'll bet this is a box of sweets."

"How did you know?" the little girl asked.

"Oh, just a wild guess," the teacher answered.

The next gift was from the son of the liquor store owner. The teacher held the package overhead, but it was leaking. She touched a drop of the leakage with her finger and touched it to her tongue. "Is it wine?" she asked with a smile.

"No-o-o-o," the boy replied with some excitement.

The teacher repeated the process, taking a larger drop of the leakage to her tongue. "Is it champagne?" she asked.

"No-o-o-o-o," the boy replied again with even greater excitement.

The teacher took one more taste before declaring, "I give up. What is it?"

With great glee the little boy shouted, "It's a puppy!"

You spend a lot of parenthood on the sidelines, loving from a distance, sensing your heart twist and turn with delight and regret while your child is happily and properly oblivious of what you're enduring.

It will be like this for the next twenty years, and someday I'll probably accept it, this rule of parenthood as fixed as a law of physics: From your child's point of view, it's never okay when you leave, but it's always okay when she does.[10]

A mother watched as her daughter hopped off the school bus and scampered toward her house in a pouring rainstorm. As the little girl ran toward the house, a lightning bolt flashed and the little girl stopped, looked up toward the sky and smiled, then began running back toward the house.

Another lightning bolt flashed, and again the little girl stopped, looked toward the sky, and smiled before running once more toward the open door of her house.

When the little girl finally arrived in the house, her mother immediately asked about her strange behavior. "Why did you keep stopping and smiling at the sky?" she asked her daughter.

"I had to, Mommy," the little girl explained. "God was taking my picture."

Raising teenagers is like nailing Jell-O to the wall.

Two things every mom needs: Velcro arms and a Teflon heart.

[Moms] are the world's greatest actresses. We have to act as if our heart isn't breaking when our child comes home from school crying because he doesn't have any friends. And yet we will never receive an Academy Award. . . . We are the most overworked and underpaid occupation there is. And yet, we are the most important.[11]

You had my mother give birth to me. You made me trust you while I was just a baby. I have leaned on you since the day I was born; you have been my God since my mother gave me birth.

—PSALM 22:9–10 NCV

# How to Be a Joyful Woman— Take Up Acting

*Practicing Random Acts of Intelligence*
*and Senseless Acts of Self-Control*

Several friends from around the country recently sent me the same wire service article they had clipped from newspapers in their area. The first paragraph warned, "Speaking in public may be more than just terrifying. The stress may be deadly."[1] The article cited a study that had shown "public speaking is a particularly potent trigger" of a dangerous heart problem.

For some folks, the fear of public speaking may cause "risky mental stress," as the article predicts, but it just doesn't work that way for me. Once I'm onstage, I feel as if a blanket of love is surrounding me as I look out and see all those upturned faces so eagerly waiting to hear my message. Nervousness and fear just aren't a problem for me.

But there have been a few exceptions recently. For instance, last spring when I got to introduce Precious Moments creator Sam Butcher to a large audience in Kansas City, I was surprised to find my heart pounding away and my palms getting sweaty. For a moment there I even thought I felt my knees knocking together! *So this is what it feels like to be terrified in front of a microphone*, I thought.

Another time when Marilyn Meberg and I were speaking together at a conference, Marilyn kept swatting at a very persistent fly that continually buzzed around her head as she spoke. When it was my turn to speak, the same fly was doing his aerial antics in front of my face, and when I caught a big breath to join in the laughter, I sucked the little bug right down my windpipe! I coughed and sputtered—and then plucked a tiny little wing off the tip of my tongue.

Such incidents make for some memorable moments. But the real stress-maker I encounter as a public speaker doesn't occur while I'm standing on the stage. The stress comes from the problems I have trying to *get* to the stage—or to the city or the hotel or the arena. Some of the crazy escapades we've managed to survive make me agree with the guy who said, "I don't mind traveling—except when I have to be away from home!"

Here are a few glimpses into the life of this over-the-hill road warrior:

One time Bill and I were flying into Memphis, and our plane arrived hours late—after midnight. There was no transportation to the hotel—all the taxis had apparently gone to roost for the night. The only good thing that happened—and it was one of those mixed blessings—was that we had no luggage to drag around in our weary state. Our luggage was lost! By the time we got to the hotel and into our room, we were both exhausted. Still, I had trouble deciding what to wear to bed since we had no luggage. I just never was one to sleep in my underwear, so instead I wrapped a big bath towel around my torso and held it in place with three of the big, round button pins I carry with me—the ones that say, "Someone Jesus loves has AIDS." It wasn't the most comfortable night I'd ever spent, but mercifully, it was short!

The Women of Faith tour arranges contracts with local transportation companies to shuttle the conference speakers, singers, and staff members between airports and hotels in the various cities. Sometimes we ride in a van or a regular car;

other times a limo shows up. (Frankly, the limos are the
vehicles I like the least. They have enough seats to haul a sym-
phony orchestra—but only enough trunk space to accommodate the piccolos!)

The handsome young limo driver who met us at the San
Antonio airport told us his "real" job as a firefighter made
moonlighting for the limo service a perfect second job for
him, since as a firefighter he knew the city like the back of his
hand. We chatted pleasantly as he drove us to our hotel. As he
whipped the big car into the hotel's circle drive, bellmen scur-
ried to open doors and help us crawl out of the backseat.
While they hurriedly began unloading the six heavy pieces of
luggage belonging to Bill, my helper, and me, we hustled into
the lobby to check in. The hotel was a grand old palace, with
beautiful oak paneling and historic markers and all sorts of
impressive fixtures. We were thrilled to get to stay in such a
remarkable place!

At the front desk, I smiled at the clerk and told her my
name. She typed it into her computer, frowned slightly, then
typed some more.

"What did you say your name was, ma'am?" she asked.

"Barbara Johnson—I'm one of the speakers at the Women
of Faith conference," I said happily, flashing her my best
smile.

She typed and scowled some more.

"What conference was that again, ma'am?"

"The Women of Faith conference—we're all staying here.
You should have lots of reservations for the conference. The
others should already be here."

The desk clerk swallowed hard and finally raised her eyes
to look carefully into my face, probably checking for signs of
senility. Slowly she asked, "Ma'am? What hotel do you think
you're at?"

"Why, the Hyatt!" I said confidently.

There was a pause as the poor woman arranged her face
into an apologetic and sympathetic smile.

"Ma'am, this hotel is the Menger."

Our limo driver—who knew the city like the back of his hand and who, by this time, had driven off into the sunset—had left us at the wrong hotel! And there was no way our six suitcases and three hefty-size bodies would fit in an ordinary taxi to get to the Hyatt, some blocks away. So there we stood, back in the circle drive with our mountain of bags, looking like befuddled pilgrims who'd just missed the bus of life. As we waited forlornly, the bellman frantically tried to find someone who could haul us away to the Hyatt.

In Detroit, we made it to the right hotel—with our luggage—at the right time. But a primary water main had been cut, and the whole suburb was without water. Immediately, I developed an overwhelming thirst and felt myself shriveling up in what I assumed was fatal dehydration. The conference would have to be canceled, we were told. The fire marshal refused to let us occupy the arena when there was no water to fight any fires that might occur. But the prayers went up, and the blessings came down, and enough water pressure was restored just in time for the event to go on as planned. The only thing different was the signs posted in all the rest rooms, warning the women that the water in the sinks and toilets was not drinkable!

In Atlanta we were thrilled to stay on the forty-second floor of one of the tallest hotels in America—thrilled, that is, until a 911 call from a hotel guest caused the elevators to be locked down in emergency mode. It happened just as hundreds of conference women were returning to the hotel after the evening session. Luci, Patsy, Marilyn, and I walked into the lobby to be met by a huge wall of women, waiting wearily for the elevators to be turned back on. The quick-witted Luci immediately sized up the situation and shouted, "Dibs on the devo!" (We're all constantly looking for new material to go in the books of devotions—we call them "devos"—that we write together every year.)

Somehow one of the gals found an express elevator that would stop only on the upper floors, beginning with the level three floors above ours. We squeezed in, rode up, and then walked down the three flights of stairs. (Tell Luci you saw it here first!)

These are just a few of the highlights. There are many more—like the sweet, helpful hostess who showed up in a sporty two-door coupe to chauffeur my two plus-size helpers and me along with our various suitcases and boxes from the hotel to the arena. What a sight we were when it was time to unload! Folks gathered around, thinking it was one of those circus acts where assorted boxes and bags come hurtling out of a tiny Volkswagen, followed by a seemingly impossible stream of big-bodied clowns.

In another city we were assigned a thoughtful hostess who was afraid to drive in traffic, so she brought along her husband—who (like so many other husbands) refused to ask for directions and got completely lost on the way to the arena.

In Birmingham, our hostess thoughtfully whisked us out to a huge suburban shopping mall for thirty minutes of "aerobic shopping" on Friday afternoon before the conference. We were so eager to get inside and discover all there was to see, we failed to note which door we had entered! So when it was time to meet the hostess back at that same door, we had no idea where it was or even what store it was in! Completely befuddled, all I could think to tell the kind officer who tried to help us was that I vaguely remembered seeing a mannequin in a purple dress. . . .

Now, none of these incidents were any fun while we were *living* them, but it's sure fun to *relive* them now—knowing we survived! As each new travelogue misadventure unfolds, it's much easier to keep a smile on my face when I focus on the fun I'll have in telling the story—just as soon as the chaos and calamity end.

### The Sandwich Stage

Whether you're a traveler or a stay-at-home woman, you probably have your own sources of stress and chaos. Some of the most overstressed women these days are those who find themselves sandwiched between the exhausting job of tending their own children while also dealing with parents who are suffering health problems or slipping into dementia—and who sometimes live hundreds or even thousands of miles away. Throw in a full-time career and/or a husband who's dealing with a similar set of parent problems, and you've got the perfect launch pad for a trip to instant insanity!

Sometimes during this stage you don't have a lot of choices about how you spend your time. You simply stumble along from one crisis to the next. There are hundreds of women out there like the one who told me her husband was out of the country on business and she had been rushing to finish a big project at work when her widowed mother, who lived a thousand miles away, required emergency surgery. The woman slept on a little cot in her mother's hospital room for several days, struggling to complete her work assignment with a laptop computer and cell phone while also tending to her mom and dealing with her two teenagers' needs—places to stay while she was away plus rides to school, church, and soccer practice—from halfway across the country. While she was there she got word that her sister-in-law, who lived alone in a city another thousand miles away, had life-threatening cancer and was also undergoing emergency surgery. Then one of her kids called and nonchalantly told her he'd gotten his tongue pierced and that the family cat had been acting strange and now refused to come out from behind the refrigerator. The refrigerator had stopped working, they hadn't heard the cat meowing in quite a while, he said, and they feared the worst.

When we're trapped in these impossible predicaments we don't have a lot of choices. Our lives seem to be controlled by whatever blow hits us next, sending us lurching from headache to heartache to horror story. But we *can* choose how we respond emotionally. We *can* choose to hold on to the One who promises never to leave us, no matter how insane our schedules get.

And we can choose to laugh.

Now, I know very well that being a joyful woman can

sometimes be a challenge. But it's like that little message someone imagined coming from God:

> I didn't say it would be easy.
> I said it would be worth it!

What I'd really like to do when the plane is late or the luggage is lost or the elevators aren't working is get upset—start whining and moaning. Other times I want to be mad; I want to raise my voice, harden my heart, tighten up my face, and unload a sharp tongue-lashing to whatever unfortunate soul happens to cross my path at that moment. But, frankly, I've tried those choices and neither one is satisfying. Oh, sure, there's a momentary release of pressure as I vent my frustration and speak my mind. But just as quickly I regret my thoughtless words and harsh remarks.

And yet, I can't remember *ever* regretting a kind word I somehow managed to share in tense times. Or a smile I forced onto my lips when I really wanted to scowl. Or a giggle that bubbled up instead of a complaint.

## A Matter of Perspective

One of the people I admire most when it comes to laughing in the face of misery is my friend Joni Eareckson Tada. What a gift she has for bringing joy into the most trying situations! Paralyzed in a diving accident, Joni has spent the last thirty-plus years in a motorized wheelchair. She writes inspiring books, paints beautiful pictures, and heads a ministry called Joni and Friends, which focuses on inspiring, helping, and sharing God's love with other wheelchair-bound Christians around the world.

Thank heaven Joni was with us at a California venue when another "misadventure"—actually quite a serious problem— occurred during a Women of Faith conference. Somehow a misunderstanding had occurred, and the conference was seriously oversold. As a result, hundreds of women showed up to attend the conference—and found *other* women already sitting in their assigned seats—and holding ticket stubs to prove they were right! The conference coordinators put out a frantic call for chairs and eventually managed to borrow some narrow, hard folding chairs from a funeral home. The seats were hastily arranged in a dark basement area of the arena, and television monitors were wheeled in so the women could see—if they had really good eyes!

As you might imagine, there were quite a few impatient and disgruntled women in that crowded room! After all, they had bought tickets like everyone else, and there they sat on those cold, hard chairs. They were still muttering when the lights were dimmed and the program began. The women in the little folding chairs leaned forward, squinting to see the monitors. Joni was the first main speaker. As she sat peacefully in her wheelchair, the tiny elevator beside the stage silently lifted her up to the platform. She motored out to the center of the stage and smiled into the cameras, greeting the thousands of listeners with her melodic alto voice.

"I hear that some of you aren't too happy with your chairs tonight," she said with a warm smile. She slowly rotated her wheelchair so she could look out at the audience all the way around her. "I certainly understand your feelings," she continued, her smile never waning. "I *hate* my chair!"

There was a little collective gasp from the audience as Joni's words sank in while all eyes took in the sight of her frail, slim body strapped into the wheelchair. "And you know what?" Joni asked, her eyes twinkling merrily. "I have a thousand friends who would *gladly* change chairs with you right now!"

Suddenly the tension was eased in the vast auditorium— and in the dark, cramped basement—and twenty thousand women had a new perspective on the evening.

Joni's words that night remind me of a story someone sent to me. It described a successful young executive who tried a new shortcut on his way to work one morning and ended up getting lost in a forsaken neighborhood of abandoned store-fronts and bleak-looking tenements. He was nervous about driving his sleek new sports car through the ghetto, and he

## KUDZU

was frustrated because instead of saving time he now would be late for work.

Suddenly a brick sailed out from between two abandoned cars with no tires that were parked at the curb. The executive slammed on the brakes, threw the car into reverse, and angrily spun the sports car back to the spot where the brick had been thrown. A skinny adolescent stood on the sidewalk, waiting expectantly for the man to roll down the window.

"What do you think you're doing?" the man shouted angrily at the kid. Just *what* are you doing?" Building up a head of steam, he ranted on, "You just put a five-thousand-dollar dent in my new car, kid! I hope you enjoyed throwing that brick, cause it's gonna cost you a lot of money!"

"Please, mister," the boy replied. "I didn't know what else to do!"

That's when the man noticed the tears sliding down the boy's cheeks and dripping off his chin. "It's my brother, mister," he said. "We was goin' to school, but he rolled off the curb and fell out of his wheelchair behind that car there, and I can't lift him up." Now sobbing, the boy asked the executive, "Would you please help me get him back into his wheelchair? He's hurt, and he's too heavy for me."

Stunned, the young executive jumped from the sleek sports car and hurried to where the brother lay crumpled in a storm drain set into the curb. He easily lifted the young boy back into the wheelchair, a dilapidated contraption with one bent wheel and a rip in the back of the vinyl seat. He wiped the lad's scrapes and cuts with his handkerchief and gently checked him over to make sure he was okay. Once the problem was fixed, the two boys' tears evaporated. The man was amazed to hear the pair giggling and teasing each other as they prepared to resume their trip to the nearby school, a sad-looking bunker-like structure surrounded by a stark concrete playground and an eight-foot-high chain-link fence.

The man watched the younger boy push his brother down the sidewalk, stunned to hear their merry chatter resume so quickly after near-calamity had struck. As the pair turned the corner, the boy turned back to flash a bright smile at the man and wave his thanks.

It was a long walk back to the sports car. The man never did fix the dent in the door. He kept it there awhile to remind him of the new perspective the boys had given him. Eventually the thrill of driving the car evaporated, and he traded it in for a pickup. He often takes the same shortcut to work, but now he takes his time, always watching for two young boys, one pushing the other in a wheelchair. He remembers the bent wheel and the torn backrest, and if he should see them again, he wants to be ready to help.

The boys in that story gave the busy executive the same gift Joni instantly shared with all the women at the conference who found themselves in an uncomfortable situation. With a bright smile and gentle words, she showed us again how to "count it all joy."[2]

What kind of perspective do *you* bring to unpleasant situations? Do you add to the gloom or introduce joy? Do you join in the grumbling or find something to laugh about? Do you follow our Lord's example and lift the spirits of "those bent beneath their loads"?[3]

### Three Little Words

One of my favorite periodicals is the wonderful little *Bits &*

*Pieces* booklet that comes in the mail fourteen times a year. A recent *Bits & Pieces* supplement was titled, "The Three Most Powerful Words in the English Language." Being quite a know-it-all when it comes to spiritual matters, I assumed the words were "I love you" or "God is good" or even "Please, take mine." So I was surprised to learn that the three little words that were guaranteed to "work miracles in your life" were something else entirely. They were:

ACT AS IF.

The writer explained, "Act the way you want to become, and you'll become the way you act." So if you want to *be* happy, begin by *acting* as if you're happy, even when you really feel as miserable as a moth in mud!

This idea certainly isn't new. It's the same premise behind the inspired verses that say:

Though the fig tree does not bud and there are no grapes on the vines, though the olive crop fails and the fields produce no food, though there are no sheep in the pen and no cattle in the stalls, yet I will rejoice in the LORD, I will be joyful in God my Savior. The Sovereign LORD is my strength; he makes my feet like the feet of a deer, he enables me to go on the heights.[4]

Be joyful! Even when the figs don't flower, the fields are flat, and your friends fail you, put a smile on your face and praise God. That's what we try to do on the Women of Faith tour when the water main breaks, the luggage is lost, and the elevators refuse to take us to our rooms on the forty-second floor (and that's probably why last year's tour was so appropriately titled *Outrageous* Joy).

We *can* do it. We *can* sparkle with joy in the deepest, darkest basement, because the Lord is our battery pack that empowers us to smile and laugh no matter how dire our circumstances appear to be. As someone said, "God often calls us to do things that we do not have the ability to do. Spiritual discernment is knowing if God calls you to do something, God empowers you to do it."[5]

We can act as if we're enjoying the journey, even when the road is rough, the springs in the seats are broken, and the air conditioning's best efforts produce a brisk 95 degrees. That kind of attitude was the focus of this Norman Vincent Peale story that was reprinted in the *Bits & Pieces* booklet:

The famous religious leader John Wesley was terrified in a violent storm on the Atlantic as he sailed to America in the 17th century. But some people aboard the wildly tossing ship were calm and confident during the storm. Wesley was so impressed by their imperturbability that he asked their secret. It proved to be simply a serene faith in God's providential care. When Wesley sadly confessed that he did not have such faith, one of them said, "It is a simple secret. Act as if you do have such faith and in time faith of that character will take hold of you." Wesley followed the advice and ultimately developed such powerful faith that he was able to overcome the most difficult situations.[6]

One of the best bonuses about being—or just *acting*—joyful is that inevitably the joy we share is reflected back to us just when we need it most. For me, this principle works like a boomerang that carries giggles and all sorts of other merry tidbits to my door on a daily basis. Or sometimes it's a note scribbled on a hot dog wrapper at a Women of Faith conference and left for me at my book table. One of my favorites was an anonymous note left by a twenty-seven-year-old woman who wanted me to know how happy it made her to join me (and the other twelve thousand women at that conference) in singing "I'll Fly Away" at the end of my talk. It really *is* inspiring to hear all those voices joyfully singing, "When I die, hallelujah, by and by, I'll fly away." This woman wrote:

Just wanted to tell you how big of a smile was on my face as we sang "I'll Fly Away." . . . Not only did I know that song, but I knew it in a way like nobody else knows it. I remember when we learned that song in church. My mom leaned over and told us the story of my grandmother singing "I'll Fly Away" at the top of her lungs. When she got to the chorus, she had forgotten the words, but that didn't stop her. She just improvised and kept right on singing. Here's her version:
I'll fly away, oh glory, I'll fly away.
*When I do, hallelujah, doo-dee-doo,*
I'll fly away!
My sisters and I will sing it that way 'til the day we "do." (I mean "die"!)

Since then, every time I've led audiences around the country in that rousing chorus, I imagine that spunky little grandma singing her own enthusiastic lyrics at the top of her lungs, and once again, my own heart is filled with joy.

Another joy gift came to me all the way from the Bahamas. When I opened the envelope, a piece of fabric fell out. Patterned with bright red blossoms spilling over straw hats on a black background, the fabric was attached with straight pins

**"OH, GLORY! OH, DELIGHT!
MY ESTROGEN PATCH JUST KICKED IN!"**

to a palm-size piece of dress-shaped cardboard. The writer explained that she had read my book *Stick a Geranium in Your Hat and Be Happy* and that recently she had bought the enclosed material to make herself a dress "and did not realize until I had the dress made that it had a hat on it with flowers. So I call it my 'Stick a Geranium in My Hat' dress, in honor of you."

It was just a little thing—a piece of fabric pinned to cardboard. But it brightened my day and made me smile to imagine another joyful woman, a stranger, thousands of miles away, wearing a colorful dress and thinking happy thoughts of me.

That friend's thoughtfulness reminded me of that beautiful little song I sang as a child:

Do not wait until some deed of greatness you may do,
Do not wait to shed your light afar,
To the many duties ever near you now be true,
Brighten the corner where you are.

Brighten the corner where you are!
Brighten the corner where you are!

Someone far from harbor you may guide across the bar,
Brighten the corner where you are.[7]

## Injecting Joy

Recently I read someone's comment that "happiness is a talent."[8] And right after that, I came upon philosopher William James's advice that said, "If you want a quality, act as if you already have it."[9] Even if you think you don't have a talent for happiness, *act* as if you do. You'll find that joy is like a vaccine that immunizes you against all sorts of maladies. Joy opens our hearts to see God's power at work in ourselves and in our world. It helps us remember God's positive answers for all the negative things we say about ourselves, as shown in this wonderful list someone sent to me:

*You say, "It's impossible."* God says, "All things are possible" (Luke 18:27).

*You say, "I'm too tired."* God says, "I will give you rest" (Matt. 11:28–30).

*You say, "Nobody really loves me."* God says, "I love you" (John 3:16, 34).

*You say, "I can't go on."* God says, "My grace is sufficient" (2 Cor. 12:9; Ps. 91:15).

*You say, "I can't figure things out."* God says, "I will direct your steps" (Prov. 3:5–6).

*You say, "I can't do it."* God says, "You can do all things" (Phil. 4:13).

*You say, "I'm not able."* God says, "I am able" (2 Cor. 9:8).

*You say, "It's not worth it."* God says, "It will be worth it" (Rom. 8:28).

*You say, "I can't forgive myself."* God says, "I forgive you!" (1 John 1:9; Rom. 8:1).

*You say, "I can't manage."* God says, "I will supply all your needs" (Phil. 4:19).

*You say, "I'm afraid."* God says, "I have not given you a spirit of fear" (2 Tim. 1:7).

*You say, "I'm always worried and frustrated."* God says, "Cast all your cares on Me" (1 Peter 5:7).

*You say, "I feel so alone."* God says, "I will never leave you or forsake you" (Heb. 13:5).

Now, no one expects you to memorize all these verses overnight and make a radical change in attitude all at once. If you're like me, you'll want to taper off your whining gradually so that you don't get attitude whiplash! In the meanwhile, you might enjoy some of these silly warning signs that you've *really* reached the end of your rope:

- You don't worry when the wind blows, because you don't have anything left to blow away.

- Your dog goes home with someone else.

- You can't even afford tuition for the school of hard knocks.

- You've kept a stiff upper lip so long that rigor mortis has set in.[10]

And when the whole world seems to have turned against you, remember this advice I saw on a greeting card:

A positive attitude may not solve all your problems, but it will annoy enough people to make the effort worthwhile!

This last little quip points to the sad fact that there *are* some people living out there in the emotional tundra who just can't stand to think of anything or anyone being joyful. It's like that old joke that defined *Puritanism* as "the haunting fear that someone, somewhere, may be happy." These anti-happy people were described last year in a newspaper article that focused on a group calling itself the Secret Society of Happy People. The organization's purpose, said its founder, is "to bring happiness out of the closet." But her efforts are not always well received. In fact, the article said she had been "cursed on national television" and had even "received veiled telephone threats" from folks who just couldn't stand to be around people who are perpetually happy. Still, the lady was determined to continue her work of encouraging "the openly happy."

As an example of how the group's members spread happiness, the article described a Texas veterinarian who clips the local newspaper for photos of students honored for academic and athletic success. He then has the pictures laminated and sends them to the student's parents with "an anonymous note offering congratulations."

The man explained that "if you do something nice and the person doesn't know where it comes from, it adds a little hint of mystery."[11]

That kind of thoughtfulness was adapted by a woman who wrote to tell me that after she had read *Geranium*, she had been inspired to make Joy Boxes full of jokes, cartoons, and other laugh-getters for friends in her support group, which focused on helping its members cope with grief. "But I quickly gave you the credit for the boxes, Barb, because my name is Joy, and I didn't want them to think I was so vain I'd name this treasure box after myself!" The woman's goal is "to be a source of encouragement to others," she wrote. "I look for ways to bring cheer. I find as I lift them up I'm at the same time lifting my own spirits."

## Turning Heartache to Joy

Sometimes the smallest gesture of joy can mean a lot to a person in pain. One woman wrote to say that her friend had given her a potted geranium for Christmas several years ago. The friend wanted a little something extra to go with the gift, so she purchased a "cute little minibook" with the word *geranium* in the title, the woman said. That book was *Stick a Geranium in Your Hat and Be Happy.*

"The little book was intended as a joke, Barb," the woman wrote. "I don't think my friend knew anything about you at the time; she just bought the book because the title went with the gift. But God intervened, and I've been a fan of yours ever since," she added. "You have a tremendous testimony to have been through so much heartbreak and then turn it into the joy of helping others. I've thanked my friend so many times for that little book she meant as a joke."

After my friend Roger Shouse worked at my book table during the Kansas City conference, he shared another idea that he and his wife, Debbie, had used to spread *Geranium*-style joy. He made up a flyer that described "How to Host Your Own Geranium Party." It listed these six simple steps:

1. Invite several ladies from your church or neighborhood. Have each bring a favorite flower.

2. Make a few simple refreshments.

3. Share your favorite story or quote from Barbara's books.

4. Show one of Barbara's videos.

5. Discuss how the value of friends and the power of prayer can help when you are hurting.

6. Exchange flowers before everyone leaves.

No, it's not always easy being a joyful woman. Most of us are more experienced in grumbling than glowing. But to those who've learned to "count it all joy," the boomerang blessings far outnumber the bruises. When you feel as if you're wandering aimlessly in the wilderness of some grief-filled desert, look around you—and find the manna for joy that God has provided. Life isn't always what we want, but it's what we've got. So, with God's help, *choose* to be joyful.

# Squirts & Squints

May your joys be added,
Your sorrows subtracted,
Your friends multiplied,
And your enemies divided.

### Kinder, Gentler Ways to Indicate Stupidity:

She's a few fries short of a Happy Meal.
He has an intellect rivaled only by garden tools.
She's a few peas short of a casserole.
He's a few feathers short of a whole duck.
In her brain, the wheel's spinning, but the hamster's dead.
His antenna doesn't pick up all the channels.
Her telephone is permanently off the hook.
His belt doesn't go through all the loops.
Her slinky's kinked.

*Rejected greeting card verse:*
My tire was thumping; I thought it was flat;
When I looked at the tire I noticed your cat. Sorry!

### Fun Things to Do in an Elevator:

1. Crack open your briefcase or purse, and while peering inside ask: "Got enough air in there?"
2. Offer nametags to everyone getting on the elevator. Wear yours upside down.
3. Stand silent and motionless in the corner, facing the wall, without getting off.

4. When arriving at your floor, grunt and strain to yank the doors open then act embarrassed when they open by themselves.
5. Greet everyone getting on the elevator with a warm handshake. Look them in the eye and say, "Welcome aboard! Just call me admiral."
6. Bet the other passengers you can fit a quarter up your nose.
7. Say "Ding!" as you pass each floor.
8. Draw a little square on the floor with chalk and announce to the other passengers that this is your personal space.

Did you ever stop to think . . .
and forget to start up again?

She who laughs last
thinks the slowest.

Sign posted on harried shopkeeper's door:
　　Out of my mind.
　　Be back in five minutes.

May God's joy shine down on you like the rays of the sun, filling your heart, soothing your spirit, and easing your pain.

(But be sure to wear some kind of joy-screen; you wouldn't want to get overjoyed.)

Success is not measured by how high you fly but how high you bounce.[12]

The flight attendant asked a passenger if he would like to have dinner.

"What are my choices?" the passenger asked.

"Yes or no," the flight attendant replied.[13]

If ignorance is bliss,
why aren't more people happy?

The young man was at the end of his rope. Seeing no way out, he dropped to his knees in prayer. "Lord, I can't go on," he said. "I have too heavy a cross to bear."

The Lord replied, "My son, if you can't bear its weight, just place your cross inside this room. Then pick out any cross you wish."

The man was filled with relief. "Thank You, Lord!" he sighed, and he did as he was told.

Inside the room, he saw many crosses, some so large the tops were not visible. Then he spotted a tiny cross leaning against a far wall.

"I'd like that one, Lord," he whispered.

The Lord replied, "My son, that's the cross you just brought in."

My next house will have no kitchen—
Just vending machines.

Oh, no! Not another learning experience!

Do you want to say you love me?
Say it now, while I can hear
Your voice, soft, low, and soothing,
Gently telling me I'm a dear.

Do you want to show you love me?
Hold my hand, caress my cheek,
And then just listen—only listen—
To my thoughts and hurts and dreams.

Age will change us, time will turn us,
Death will take us all too soon.
Do you want to say you love me?
Say it now. I'll say it too.

—ANN LUNA

Lord Jesus Christ,
You are the journey,
the journey's end,
the journey's beginning.

—DEAN MAYNE,
FORMER DEAN OF
WESTMINSTER ABBEY

The Lamb . . . will be their shepherd; he will lead them to
springs of living water. And God will wipe away every tear
from their eyes.

—REVELATION 7:17

# I Finally Got My Head Together—
# Then My Body Fell Apart!

## *I'm Just a Raggedy Ann in a*
## *Barbie Doll World*

**W**e all felt so sorry for the clerk working the front desk at our hotel when the Women of Faith speakers checked in year before last in Charlotte. She worked very quickly to make sure our check-in went smoothly on that Thursday night before the Women of Faith conference. Her gracious greeting made us feel completely welcome. We got the feeling she'd been there a long time, because she seemed to know every-thing about the hotel and everyone who worked in it. But, bless her heart, she was *very* pregnant. We women groaned, thinking how her back must hurt and her feet had to swell by the end of eight hours standing behind the counter. She didn't seem a bit weary as she checked us in, though. In fact, the merriest sparkle shone out from her eyes. She seemed to con-stantly be on the verge of bursting out in laughter.

Yes, she was a very charming young lady, as sweet as she could be. There was just one rather tragic thing that made our hearts ache with sympathy as we watched her work. She had a *very* noticeable facial-hair problem! Above her upper lip there was a thin, dark mustache that was easily visible from across the lobby. In fact, it looked like she might have tried to trim it a little to keep the tips of the hairs out of her mouth!

*What a shame!* I thought. *She's such a pretty young woman— but that mustache! Someone should tell her about electrolysis or that new laser hair-removal treatment.*

I even thought about taking up a little collection from the Women of Faith folks, but I just couldn't figure out how I could present the gift to her without hurting her feelings. It just didn't seem very courteous to shove an envelope at her and say, "Here, Honey. Go get your lip waxed."

So we didn't do anything about it—except discuss how noticeable it was to us and how someone who's in front of the public all day, as she was, must surely get some rude stares and even harsh remarks. We felt sorry for her soon-to-be-born child, knowing the poor kid would be teased by insensitive classmates about having a mother with a mustache.

We didn't see her again for the rest of the visit. But when we were at the front desk again on Sunday morning, rushing to get checked out and head for the airport, there was something about the desk clerk that once again bothered me. Something I couldn't quite put my finger on. He was a young, handsome man with sparkly eyes, a bright smile, and—good grief! He had the same thin, dark mustache above his upper lip that the pregnant woman had had on Thursday!

"There you go, Mrs. Johnson. You're all set to go," he said, sliding my receipt across the counter and flashing that same bright smile his pregnant twin had given me three days earlier. My eyes must have bulged out of my head like gourds. I *know* my mouth dropped open, because he asked politely, "Is there something else?"

I gulped, wondering if I knew his mother. You see, my work with Spatula Ministries puts me in contact with the hurting families of homosexuals and other adult children whose lifestyles and escapades have splattered their parents on the ceiling. I hear from lots of brokenhearted mothers who write to tell me about their trials. Looking at the woman/man that morning in Charlotte, I assumed he had to be a cross-dresser or sex-change person, and the words I've preached to so many others suddenly came echoing back through my mind: *That poor, misguided boy is some dear mother's son!* I wanted to reach across the counter, wrap the young man in my arms, and say, "Honey, God loves you, no matter how strange you are."

But then I remembered that he had been *pregnant* on Thursday night. That's when my mind—what few brain cells were left at that point—*really* started to short-circuit.

Seeing my total bewilderment, the man's face wrinkled with sympathy; the lips under the mustache pursed into a cooing little "O," and he asked gently, "Are you okay?"

"You—you . . . on Thursday, you were . . . was that . . . were you . . . ?" I was totally at a loss to know how to ask this most personal of questions.

"That was me, all right," he said with a chuckle. "The hotel was having a costume contest for Halloween, and I won first prize!"

When I remember that creative young desk clerk and how we worried about her facial-hair problem, I can't help but wonder if there are folks out there who, when their paths cross mine as I travel the country, think, *Golly, she's such a nice lady. But can't she afford at least some costume jewelry instead of that rubber band she wears for a bracelet?* Or, *How could a woman who shares her message of hope with so many people be seen in public carrying a purse with ripped seams, using a wallet held together with staples, and wearing a dress with buttons attached with safety pins?*

Actually, I *know* people notice these fashion faux pas, because unlike my reluctance to mention the beauty problem to the hotel worker in Charlotte, they seem eager to point them out! For example, the lady sitting next to me on a plane recently looked over at me and said, "You surely don't *look* like a woman who would have a tattoo!"

I couldn't imagine what would make her say such a thing. Then I followed her gaze down to my right hand—and saw how I'd covered my palm with all the crucial numbers and details I needed to remember that day. It's such a bother, digging through my purse to find something to write on—and my hand is so, well, *handy!*

## HERMAN®

10-6                                    © Jim Unger/dist. by United Media, 1999

**"For the money I'm paying, I hope
you're painting the real me."**

On that day, I knew I would be needing the telephone number of the shuttle service that would take us home from the airport, so I had written it on my hand—right beside my flight number, departure gate, and the name of the shipping service that would be transporting my books to the next venue. Looking over the ink marks, I decided all the scribbles *did* look a little like a work of modern art.

And the rubber bands—I can explain that too. No, actually I can't. It's just a habit born of either frugality or laziness. Whenever I find a rubber band, I pop it onto my wrist, knowing that sooner or later I'll *need* a rubber band; I certainly don't want to waste it, and who wants to take time to find the rubber band box and put it with its stretchy brothers and sisters?

Now, my tattered tote bag . . . well, it's the perfect size and shape, and it has all these great pockets, and I've tried other styles, but they just aren't the same. You wouldn't believe how many people take pity on that tote bag—and then send me a new one, apparently thinking I can't afford a decent purse. But the thing is, I like my old tattered one best; I know right where everything is, and since the seams are ripped, it's even a little bigger now than when it was new.

And as for my wallet, yes, it has been through the mill. But I like to think the staples give it character. They certainly make it easily identifiable! Not too long ago, I lost my wallet when I was rushing through my local market picking up a few groceries. When I got to the checkout lane, I was looking for my wallet and couldn't find it. Apparently I'd laid it down in the tomatoes, where a kindhearted young couple found it wedged among the Big Boys and Beefsteaks. They turned it in to the manager just as I was entering the early stages of lost-wallet panic.

The young man and his girlfriend probably saw the worn and stained leather—not to mention the STAPLES holding it together—and thought, *Oh, some poverty-stricken and absent-minded little old lady left her pocketbook in the produce.* Then they opened it and saw my ID. When they turned it in to the store manager, the young man said, "Oh, my mom reads *all* her books!"

And then there's the matter of the safety pins that hold the buttons on some of my clothes. At one conference, a woman even offered to take my jacket and *sew* the buttons on for me when she noticed all the safety pins holding the buttons on. But I explained that on that outfit the buttons have to be taken off before it can be dry-cleaned, so I just use safety pins to make it easier!

## Fashion Foibles, Beauty Bloopers

Now, the theme of this chapter is supposed to be beauty and health, describing ways women keep themselves looking good and feeling good. But as you've probably figured out already, I'm certainly not a role model for fashion statements and attention to detail! Despite my good intentions, I rarely manage to achieve that "put-together" look. And even when I do, something happens that foils my attempts.

For example, I sometimes wear false eyelashes when I'm speaking because for some strange reason when I'm wearing false eyelashes I don't cry when I tell my story describing my husband's car accident, the deaths of two sons, and the alienation of another due to his homosexuality. It must be a psychological thing: I know if I cry, the eyelashes will come off, so I don't cry.

But sometimes the eyelashes come loose anyway! For instance, last year in Orlando, when the temperature was in the high 200s and the humidity apparently was stuck on the "rain forest" setting, the glue was melting and the eyelash was curling off my eyelid as I stepped onstage. Every time I blinked, I got a glimpse of a little wisp of hairs fluttering and flapping past my eyeball. Finally, in frustration, I just reached up, ripped it off, and threw it on the stage. Any thoughts that the eighteen thousand women in the audience wouldn't notice quickly disappeared. They roared! It got such a response I just reached up, ripped off the other one, and threw it on the floor too—so the first one wouldn't be lonely, I explained.

And while I'm confessing my personal preference for comfort over fashion, I might as well include the fact that my ten-

**Murray's Law by Leslie Moak Murray**

dency to go for practical over pretty extends to our car. It's Bill's beloved twenty-three-year-old Volvo, and it has become a regular member of our family. Like me, it's not the snazziest thing on the road, but it's familiar and comfortable and practical—and we wouldn't think of parting with it. (Well, that's not exactly true. We've given it away twice, but like a devoted dog, it just keeps coming back to us.)

Please don't send me a new wallet or eyelashes guaranteed to stick or a notepad to wear on a string around my neck so I don't have to write on my hand. And while I appreciate the purple luggage—a complete set!—that a friend gave me last year after seeing my tattered tote bag and my dependable old black suitcase (which I've decorated with bright yellow tape so I can spot it easily on the baggage carousel), I *don't* need new stuff! I just need to be left alone to grow older with my *old* stuff!

Probably by now you've gotten the message that I won't be imparting great fashion hints and trendy beauty secrets here, but I *will* try my best to give you something that works even better to improve your appearance: a smile. And since my favorite form of aerobics is belly laughing, you'll get your exercise too. We'll throw in a quick faith lift, and before you know it, you may undergo a total-body makeover!

Let's start with these "time-tested inexpensive beauty hints" from writer Sam Levenson:

> For attractive lips, speak words of kindness.
> For lovely eyes, seek out the good in people.
> For a slim figure, share your food with the hungry.
> For beautiful hair, let a child run his fingers through it
>    once a day.
> For poise, walk with the knowledge that you'll never
>    walk alone.[1]

Those words describe a much better way to improve our appearance than the negative (but, I'll admit, *funny*) method someone sent to me in a card:

Remember these two simple steps to enhance your appearance:

1. Buy an expensive, full-length coat.
2. Never, ever take it off!

My philosophy is that we should just do our best—and laugh about the rest. We have to keep things in perspective. Sure we may be fat, ugly, and have the fashion sense of Phyllis Diller, but as long as our sense of humor is visible, we'll manage the rest!

**Ralph**

"Is your blow-dryer still broken?"

## Too Big for Our Britches—and Our Dresses

Why do we complain so about our body shapes and sizes and want to keep them hidden under wraps? And anyway, how did those single-digit sizes become all the rage? Beauty seemed a lot more realistic—and attainable—when terms like *voluptuous* and *ample* were more common than the dreaded words *lean* and *firm*. For many of us, it's quite comforting to remember that Marilyn Monroe wore a size 12 and that even though there *are* a handful of supermodels who wear a size 8, there are three billion women on the planet who don't! In fact, it was reported recently that the average American woman weighs 144 pounds and wears a 12 or 14. Another survey reported that 70 percent of all adults in the United States are overweight.

It seems ironic that while the models in the fashion magazines are getting thinner, so many other things are getting bigger. Maybe it's because serving sizes in restaurants are expanding along with everything else. As one writer said about restaurant and fast-food trends, "Food is huge. A simple plate of pasta is now a trough of tortellini. . . . Bagels are the size of throw pillows."[2] Another writer suddenly realized she was eating a whole day's calories—at breakfast. After consuming a muffin the size of a cake and a "bagel on growth hormones" she could only moan, "Thank God for the hole in the middle!"[3]

Drinks are getting bigger too. Just think how soda pop servings have grown from the original six-ounce bottle of Coca-Cola. Now convenience stores offer gargantuan, sixty-four-ounce Bladder Busters that are big enough to quench the thirst of a minivan full of Boy Scouts—but are intended for just one person.

(And speaking of filling up the minivan passengers, consider the news that future cars may have everything from microwave ovens and temperature-controlled cup holders to built-in trash compactors and fold-up tray tables. Pretty soon we'll be taking our kitchens with us everywhere we go! Imagine what *that* will do to our attempts at dieting!)

THAT NEW DIET DRUG IS MARVELOUS! OF COURSE, THERE ARE SIDE EFFECTS!

Either we need to learn to eat less despite the monster-size packaging and the mobile kitchen trends, or we need to move to Africa, where in some countries "culture-conscious people . . . hail a woman's rotundity as a sign of good health, prosperity, and allure." In fact, teenage girls are sometimes tucked away in "fattening rooms" for several months where their only goal is to acquire "the traditional mark of female beauty . . . : *fat*."[4]

For most of us, moving to Africa is out of the question. Many women head instead to the plastic surgeon. Someone sent me a joke recently about a self-conscious woman in her late forties who was rushed to the hospital suffering a heart attack. Despite the medical team's best efforts, the woman's heart failed. She felt herself hurtling down a long, dark tunnel toward a piercing beam of light. At the end, she heard a voice say, "It is not your time. Go back."

"When will it be my time?" the woman asked.

"You will live another forty-three years, eight months, and seven days."

"Oh, thank you!" she cried.

Dramatically revived in the emergency room, the woman asked her doctors if she could stay in the hospital a while longer. She had more than forty-three years left to live, and she wanted to look her best. "Call the plastic surgeons," she said. "I want *everything* done!"

For three weeks she remained in the hospital and had a complete makeover: an eyelift, neck tightening, tummy tuck, thigh liposuction, bottom lift—you name it, she had it. When she finally recovered she walked out of the hospital a new woman—and was immediately struck by an ambulance and killed.

Meeting God again at the end of the tunnel, the woman fumed, "What happened? You told me I was going to live another forty-three years, eight months, and seven days!"

God shrugged and answered, "I didn't recognize you!"

The time we wish the hardest that we could make our bodies unrecognizable is when we're trying on swimsuits. The ordeal is perfectly described in this little essay by an unknown writer. While the writer's name isn't known, her attitude could be mine:

I have just survived the annual torture and humiliation of buying a new swimsuit. For generations, bathing suits for mature, "full-figured" women have been no-nonsense garments that showed an understanding that the word *full* did not mean *overflowing*. These bathing suits were boned, cupped, underwired, overwired, and reinforced— true feats of engineering rather than whims of fickle fashion. In those days, a bathing suit was built to hold up, lift up, and tuck in, and it did a darn good job.

Today's swimsuits are designed for malnourished pre-pubescent girls with pencil-shaped figures carved from granite. And even though these nymphs have no flab whatsoever, they wear swimsuits made from space-age material with enough tensile strength to launch satellites into orbit.

The mature, full-figured woman has only two options: She can either show up at the maternity department and try on a flounsey floral swimsuit with a skirt, looking like the dancing hippopotamus in Disney's *Fantasia*, or she can wander, shell-shocked, through the department store swimwear section trying to make a sensible selection from a tangled assortment of what looks like brightly col-ored rubber bands.

I tried my luck in the department store and thought I heard, as I neared the fitting rooms, the distinct sound of wailing and gnashing of teeth. Inside the chamber of hor-rors I fought my way into the swimsuit, wishing a stout girlfriend or my husband could have been there to help me wage the battle. I was exhausted by the time I finally twanged the shoulder strap into place—then gasped in horror as I turned to face the mirror. I thought I'd some-how managed to turn my head all the way around to my back: My bosoms had disappeared! Eventually I found one of them smooshed under my left armpit and, after several minutes of searching, located the other one flattened under my ribcage at the bottom of my sternum.

Because modern bathing suits have no bra cups, the mature, full-figured woman is forced to wear her bosoms smashed across her chest like a speed bump. On the other hand—or perhaps I should say the other *end*—it takes no time at all to find the mature, full-figured woman's hips and thighs. They ooze out from beneath the bottom of the swimsuit like a box of lard that's been sat on. Sighing, I realigned my speed bump, snapped the Spandex over the escaping cellulite, and braced myself for another look in the mirror.

Actually, the suit fit perfectly. That is, it perfectly fit those parts of me that were willing to stay inside. The rest of me peeked out rebelliously from top, bottom, and sides like curious children. I resembled a lump of bread dough wrapped with garters, a tablecloth pulled through a napkin ring. . . .

Then I tried on a bright pink number with a top that resembled a cleric's collar attached to suspenders. Not

**"If only I were as young as my mirror thinks I am!"**

only did it leave 90 percent of me exposed above the waist, it had such a high-cut leg I thought I would have to wax my eyebrows to wear it.

Finally I found a swimsuit that fit. It's a simple, two-piece style with a shorts-style bottom and a halter top. It was affordable, comfortable, and flab-flattering, so I bought it.

Then I got it home and read the label, which explained why this perfect suit for mature, full-figured women had languished on the rack. The tag said, "Material may become transparent in water."

This woman's comments about what happens to her "bosoms" when she stuffs them into a Spandex swimsuit reminded me of another funny description of one of a woman's most dreaded ordeals: the mammogram.

A mammogram is an x-ray that has its own name because no one wants to actually say the word *breast*. Mammograms require your breasts to do gymnastics. If you have extremely agile breasts, you should do fine. But most breasts, however, pretty much hang around doing nothing in particular, so they are woefully unprepared. But you can prepare for a mammogram right at home with these simple exercises.

*Exercise 1:* Refrigerate two bookends overnight. Lay one of your breasts between the bookends and smash the bookends together as hard as you can. Do this three times daily.

*Exercise 2:* Locate a pasta maker or old wringer washer. Feed the breast into the machine and start cranking. Repeat twice daily.

*Exercise 3 (more advanced):* Situate yourself comfortably on your side on the garage floor. Place one of your breasts snugly behind the rear tire of the family van. When you give the signal, hubby will slowly ease the car into reverse. Hold for five seconds and repeat on the other side.[5]

**IF WOMEN CONTROLLED MEDICINE**

Now, just let me pass along one more observation some insightful woman made about breasts before we move on to other beauty tips and quips. This lady said:

I have found at my age that going braless pulls all the wrinkles out of my face.

If you *do* wear a bra, you'll want to make sure you choose the type that's right for you. It's really very simple:

- The Catholic type supports the masses,
- The Salvation Army type lifts up the fallen, and
- The Baptist type makes mountains out of molehills.

No matter what kind of bra you wear—or *if* you wear a bra at all!—the most important wardrobe you can possess is the one described in the apostle Paul's letter to the Colossians:

Therefore, as the elect of God, holy and beloved, put on tender mercies, kindness, humility, meekness, longsuffer-

ing; bearing with one another, and forgiving one another.
. . . But above all these things put on love.[6]

A kind friend sent me a beautiful little story about the
wardrobe Paul describes, and she even illustrated the story
for me. She's allowed me to adapt it to share with you here. I
hope you enjoy it as much as I did.

*The apostle Paul listed garments of the Holy Spirit in
his letter to Colossian believers. First on his list is tender mercies. Also known as compassion, tender mercies
are acts of empathy for weak or hurting people. They
are usually motivated by feeling the same kind of pain
as others or being able to imagine it. I call tender mercies the underwear of God's wardrobe—personal and
next to the skin. They are the foundation for everything
that goes on the outside.*

*Next on Paul's list is kindness—a warm-
hearted deed as simple as a smile. But kindness
is more than that. It's an attitude that involves
treating others with honor and significance. The
attitude of kindness is everyday stuff like
a great pair of sneakers. Not frilly. Not
fancy. Just plain and comfortable.*

*Humility is next. No matter how much we win or
lose in life, God wraps us in a beautiful cloak of grace.
When we're humiliated, He loves us exactly as we
are. When we're in the limelight, we understand
the big part He played in our success.*

*Meekness is one of my favorite things to wear. Some
people think it's non-descript, but I disagree. Meekness makes it possible to endure difficult circumstances and poor treatment at the hands of others. It
is a durable garment with interesting textures. And
meekness looks different on everyone!*

*How about long-suffering? Sometimes I wish that old rag would just wear out so I could get something more glamorous and colorful. But I know God has fashioned even this to enhance my life. There are times when long-suffering is the only appropriate thing to wear for a particular occasion—and then I'm glad it's in the closet.*

*Bearing with others and forgiveness are the outerwear of God's designs. They are the things we wear on top of everything else before we go out into the world. Without them we would get awfully cold. They protect us from the harsh elements and keep icy wind from blowing down our necks. As we face difficult circumstances, we button them up often and keep on trudging.*

*Above all else, Paul says, put on love. Without love, we are never fully dressed in Christ's wardrobe. You might think of love as your best hat or the jeweled pin on the lapel of life. It is that one essential accessory you should never leave behind. Never go anywhere without love![7]*

## Squirts & Squints

I have a great diet.
You're allowed to eat anything you want,
but you must eat it in the company of naked fat people.

The second day of a diet is always easier than the first.
By the second day you're off it.

A preacher visited an elderly woman from his congregation. As he sat on the couch he noticed a large bowl of peanuts on the coffee table. "Mind if I have a few?" he asked.

"No, not at all," the old woman replied.

They chatted for an hour, and as the preacher stood to leave, he realized that instead of eating just a few peanuts, he had emptied most of the bowl. "I'm so sorry for eating all your peanuts," he said. "I really just meant to eat a few."

"Oh, that's all right," replied the woman. "Ever since I lost my teeth all I can do is suck the chocolate off them."

I don't mind the rat race,
but I could do with a little more cheese.

Amazing! You just hang something in your closet for a while, and it shrinks two sizes.

Despite the cost of living, have you noticed how it remains so popular?

I have a friend who is fifty years old but she tells folks she's sixty—because she looks great for sixty and *awful* for fifty!

*Beauty Tip:* Beware of tucking your dress into the back of your underwear after using the rest room. You'll know this personal grooming error has occurred when you hear snickers from the people you pass on the street. Another giveaway will be the draft you feel on the back of your thighs.

Let the beauty that you love be what you do.
There are hundreds of ways to kneel and kiss the ground.

—Thirteenth-Century Poem

The Greek word for chocolate is *theobroma,*
which means "food of the gods."

If we are what we eat
then I'm easy, fast, and cheap.

**SHOE**

A balanced diet is a cookie in each hand.

*A greeting card verse we'll probably never see:*
You had your bladder removed,
now you're on the mends.
Here's a bouquet of flowers
and a box of Depends.

There are two kinds of women who will pay big bucks for a makeup mirror that magnifies their faces. The first are young models who need to be sure to cover every eyelash and define their lips. The second group are women who, without their glasses, can't even *find* their faces.

The colorful way some men describe maturing women:
Girls start out as beautiful little buds.
Next they blossom into womanhood.
Then they go on to become blooming idiots!

The easiest way to lose weight is to check it as airline baggage.[8]

If I had a beauty shop I'd name it this:
Curl Up and Dye

A telephone greeting I hope I never hear:
"Thank you for calling Incontinence Hotline. Can you hold please?"

### Medical Daffinitions

*Artery:* the study of paintings

*Bacteria:* back door to cafeteria

*CAT scan:* search for kitty

*Dilate:* to live long

*Hangnail:* what you hang your coat on

*Node:* was aware of

*Outpatient:* a person who has fainted

*Recovery room:* place to do upholstery

My sister and I bought fake fur coats on sale at the same time. If we looked like two polar bears on a Klondike bar, no one ever mentioned it.

There are many women like me who talk about cosmetic surgery, but our philosophy prevails:

No guts—live with the ruts.

When we were in Dallas, I saw many women wearing shirts identifying themselves as S.H.E.E.P. from the Garland, Texas, Tree of Life Church. I knew I would fit right in when one member told us the letters stand for "Sisters Helping, Encouraging, *Eating,* and Praying."

I like to think Psalm 16:6 (KJV) is talking about laugh lines and good genes rather than land boundaries: "The lines are fallen unto me in pleasant places; yea, I have a goodly heritage."

# We Started Out with Nothing— and Still Have Most of It Left

## Martha Stewart Doesn't Live Here— Thank Goodness!

Like many couples whose children are no longer living at home, Bill and I looked around one day and realized it was time to "downsize" our household in proportion to our shrinking family. We no longer needed a house big enough to accommodate the two of us plus four sons. It was time to move on.

Someone had told me about an attractive adult community of mobile homes approximately twenty-five miles from our house, but Bill was adamant that he would never live in a "trailer camp." Still, the descriptions I'd heard of the place seemed so appealing that I kept whining until Bill finally gave in. He agreed that we could stop by the place on our way home from church one Sunday, but he warned me we wouldn't be there long because it would be a waste of time.

We pulled in the entrance and saw a sparkling lake with ducks swimming peacefully and large fountains spraying water. Then we drove down a couple of quiet streets bordered by manicured grounds that looked like the well-tended landscaping at Disneyland. An agent showed us one

of the models—and within half an hour we'd bought a new
home! Even more incredible, Bill refused to leave! He bought
a cot and a television and "moved in" *himself* that very day,
noting it was closer to his work and that he was sure I'd be
able to pack up our house and get it sold faster if he wasn't
"underfoot." This picture of leisurely living with a pool and
Jacuzzi a few feet away really enticed him.

We bought the new place in May, and by September I had
sold our home in West Covina and was ready to join Bill in his
beautiful "trailer camp." It was hard to leave the house we'd
lived in for thirty years; after all, we'd shared years of good
times in that home with our four rambunctious boys. But there
had been bad times too—really sad times as we struggled to
deal with the aftermath of Bill's accident, the deaths of two
sons, and having a third son move out and disown us after we
argued about his homosexuality.

Major life changes—like moving out of the family home—
can be traumatic for anyone. But I didn't want to be one of
those women who get so stubbornly attached to a structure of
boards and nails that they cause headaches for their children.
We know too many of these older folks who refuse to leave the
place where they've lived for decades, even if the roof is about
to fall in and the stairs are too steep to climb. We wanted a
place where we could enjoy life without having to worry about
mowing the grass or cleaning the pool. And now, more than
twenty years later, we've had no regrets about our decision to
move; we've thoroughly enjoyed our "mobile home" (actually,

**Rhymes with Orange**

© 1999 Hilary B. Price. Distributed by and reprinted with special permission of King Features Syndicate.

it's not mobile at all but *modular*). There's a convenient recreation center nearby, friendly neighbors, and very little upkeep. We love it.

Still, the experience taught me firsthand about the hassles of moving. How you military families and "upwardly mobile" couples do it so frequently is beyond my comprehension! Moving is one headache I hope never to repeat again. The only place I'm moving to is my mansion in heaven or the Home for the Bewildered down the street—either way I don't expect to do any of the heavy lifting!

When we moved, Bill and I both thought we got the hardest jobs. My job during all those months of getting things ready was to keep the house clean for visits by prospective buyers and handle the paperwork and financial matters. For Bill, our move meant hauling thirteen carloads of stuff from West Covina to La Habra. Now, I didn't really think that was too big a deal; if that had been *my* job, I would have just carried armloads of clothes, books, or whatever to the car, shoved everything in and held it until I could get the doors closed, then dumped it out in one huge pile when I got to my destination. But Bill is an engineer. So each item in each of those thirteen loads was carefully packed, precisely loaded, methodically sorted, perfectly labeled, and then systematically deposited in exactly the right place at the new house. It's a wonder we *still* aren't in the midst of moving at the rate he was going!

But his efforts certainly paid off. By the time I moved in, he had lined every drawer in the house with Armstrong vinyl sheeting, precisely cut so there were no bulges or upturned edges, and he had carefully placed all our things in perfect order throughout the house. (Of course, that didn't last long once I was there, with my rather casual housekeeping philosophy, but still, it was nice for the one day it lasted.)

It's not that I dislike organization. It's just that I am not a fanatic about housekeeping. My philosophy is: Why put something away when you're just gonna have to get it out again in a day or two? And besides, when I'm cleaning, I get distracted by every little thing. I might notice a magazine article I want to read and sit down to scan it—until a letter lying on the desk catches my eye. I move over there to see who it's from, maybe carrying it to the kitchen where the light is better. Standing in front of the sink, I notice the jagged edges of the coffeecake we shared for breakfast—and of course have to slice away just a sliver to make it look neat (and pop the trimming in my mouth, of course). You can see how difficult it is for me!

When I'm cleaning the bathtub, I might see the new bath-oil beads someone gave me and decide right then and there to see how quickly they dissolve. The next thing you know, I'm up to my chin in a bubble bath! When I do manage to stick to the task at hand, I usually try to think up ways to make it fun. Sometimes I sing silly songs or make up rhymes like this one:

> Sing a song of dustballs,
> A corner full of mold,
> Four and twenty cobwebs,
> Swinging to and fro. . . .

Apparently I'm not the only one whose mind is nudged to nonproductive creativity when it comes to doing household cleaning. Recently I saw these silly definitions and thought I should have invented them:

FRUST (n.)—The small line of debris that refuses to be swept onto the dustpan and keeps backing a person across the room until she finally gives up and sweeps it under the rug.

CARPETUATION (n.)—The act, when vacuuming, of running over a string at least a dozen times, picking it up, examining it, then putting it back down to give the vacuum cleaner one more chance.

But no matter how silly I get, it's still *work* to try to organize the chaos that seems to build around me. When it comes to coping with clutter, I share the attitude of that astronaut husband and his wife at the beginning of the movie *Apollo 13*. They've just given a wild party, and they're sitting in the backyard in the midst of the debris left by the partyers, looking up at the moon. "I can't deal with cleaning up," the wife moans, collapsing into a lawnchair. "Let's sell the house."

"Okay," her husband replies, never batting an eye.

That's one of the few good things about moving—the choice it gives you. You can decide to take all your clutter with you to fill up your next home, or you can leave a lot of it behind—given to friends or sold at garage sales. Of course, you may need "clutter counseling" before you can take the latter route and actually give up your priceless treasures so you can enjoy a new, streamlined lifestyle. For those of us who are organizationally impaired, there's a sense that clutter is cozy while neatness is neurotic.

One clutter-besieged woman told me she'd recently conquered this mental barrier and had gone on a clutter-clearing binge that produced "the mother of all garage sales." The woman cleaned out all the knickknacks displayed artistically throughout the house, eliminated all the extra linens she'd been hanging on to, and dug out all the toys her kids had hidden in their closets so many years ago. She'd even emptied the attic of all the old, ugly 1950s furniture she'd inherited from her mother—furniture she'd planned to use in the summer cottage she and her husband had hoped to build when their kids were younger. Truth be told, she'd always hated that orange vinyl sofa and Formica-topped coffee table.

So, in full yard-sale mode, she gleefully dragged everything out into the front lawn, sold it for pennies, and felt great about the whole endeavor—until the Sunday paper came. A headline in the lifestyle section proclaimed, "'Happy Days' Furnishings Are Here Again." She stopped reading after the sentence that said, "Plan on paying at least $2,000 for a 1950s sofa—*if* you can find one of the sleek, orange vinyl models in a vintage shop. And a hard-to-find Formica-topped coffee table, with its sleek, classic silhouette, may run almost as much."

Reprinted with permission of John McPherson.

**"You bonehead! That's the same lamp we sold at our garage sale last year for three dollars!"**

## Headache Hotel

It's as hard for some of us to part with clutter as it would be for us to part the Red Sea. Let's face it. We need help. Somehow it's comforting to us to know those old magazines, outgrown clothes, and hand-me-down doilies are nearby in case we ever have time to read, lose fifty pounds, or find a naked spot on a tabletop that cries out to be dressed. While I sympathize with this mind-set, I must admit I don't live this way anymore. Except for my Joy Room, which is filled with all sorts of goofy gadgets and funny plaques, my house is pretty well organized—thanks to Bill. There are downsides to this, of course. As a result of his zest for organization, I can't find anything on my own. And the instant I lay something down he snatches it up and "puts it away." If I get a glass from the cupboard, I can't set it on the counter while I turn to the refrigerator to retrieve the milk. Bill will put it away before I can fill it up!

If it weren't for the fact that I'm married to this *extremely* organized person (perhaps the only person in the world who *staples* his socks together and hopes for the best before leaving them in my laundry room), my house would be furnished in a decorating style somewhere between chaos and confusion.

But Bill's anti-clutter attitude helps keep me—and all my stuff—in line. Without him, I'd be a first-rate loser. Not that it would be my fault, of course. Things simply have a way of getting away from me. When I turn my back for a mere instant, *poof!* My glasses, pocketbook, keys, and crucial bits of paper bearing absolutely necessary numbers suddenly vanish. It's so remarkable, I expect the phenomenon to be profiled someday on the *X-Files.*

*Reprinted with permission of John McPherson.*

**"Oh that? That's so I can keep your socks
paired up in the laundry."**

The fortunate thing for me, a *loser,* is that, as people often do, I married my opposite—a *finder.* Several years ago, I clipped a magazine article written by a finder about what it was like to live with a loser. One paragraph, in particular, has helped me understand what it must be like for Bill to live with me—and the last sentence keeps me striving to become less of a loser. The writer said, "I'll say this for most of the losers I know—they are optimists. Just because they can't actually put a hand on something right this minute doesn't mean it's *lost*, for heaven's sake: probably it's only teasing, and the losers are certainly not about to waste precious energy looking for it. As I ransack drawers and closets, their air of patient perplexity is a vivid reminder of how many murders are committed in the home."[1]

### Decorated with Joy

Whatever you and your house are like—whether your house-keeping system is the casual stow-and-slam method or the super-organized home where even the dustballs line up evenly under the bed, the most important thing to fill your home with is *joy*. What a blessing it is to step inside a home and immediately feel surrounded by a bubble of laughter and a blanket of love. In my home, I've tried to make the colors blend and the furniture fit. But the most important thing is that wherever I look in our house, I see things that bring a smile to my face and warmth to my heart.

It's amazing to me to see the extremes some people go to under the guise of interior decorating and homemaking. You know you're in the home of a "decorating extremist" when you find a slice of lemon floating in the dog's water dish and all the table napkins, washcloths, and even the paper towels are folded in the shape of swans.

Last year an unknown writer composed a funny Martha Stewart parody describing this kind of silliness. When it circulated on the Internet, at least a dozen people sent me copies, knowing how far it was from *my* seat-of-the-pants decorating style. But the *really* funny part came later when a fictitious response was added by another mystery writer. In this version, the correspondence supposedly occurs between Martha Stewart and humorist Erma Bombeck.

Dear Erma,

This perfectly delightful note is being sent on paper I made myself to tell you what I have been up to. Since it snowed last night, I got up early and made a sled with old barn wood and a glue gun. I handpainted it in gold leaf, got out my loom, and made a blanket in peaches and mauves. Then to make the sled complete, I made a white horse to pull it from DNA that I just had sitting around in my craft room.

By then it was time to start making the placemats and napkins for my twenty breakfast guests. I'm serving the old standard Stewart twelve-course breakfast, but I'll let you in on a little secret: I didn't have time to make the table and chairs this morning, so I used the ones I had on hand.

Before I moved the table into the dining room, I decided to add just a touch of the holidays. So I repainted the room in pinks and stenciled gold stars on the ceiling. Then, while the homemade bread was rising, I took antique candle molds and made the dishes to use for breakfast. These were made from Hungarian clay, which you can get in almost any Hungarian craft store.

Well, I must run. I need to finish the buttonholes on the dress I'm wearing for breakfast. I'll get out the sled and drive this note to the post office as soon as the glue dries on the envelope I'll be making. Hope my breakfast guests don't stay too long. I have forty thousand cranberries to string with bay leaves before my speaking engagement at noon. It's a good thing!

Love,<br>Martha

P.S. When I made the ribbon for this typewriter, I used ⅛-inch gold gauze. I soaked the gauze in a mixture of white grapes and blackberries that I grew, picked, and crushed last week just for fun.


Dear Martha,

I'm writing this on the back of an old shopping list. Pay no attention to the coffee and jelly stains. I'm twenty minutes late getting my daughter up for school, trying to pack a lunch with one hand while talking on the phone to the dog pound with the other. Seems old Ruff needs bailing out again. Burned my arm on the curling iron when I was trying to make those cute curly fries last night. How DO they do that?

Still can't find the scissors to cut out some snow-flakes. Tried using an old disposable razor—trashed the tablecloth in the process, but at least it no longer has those annoying fuzzballs that caused the water glasses to tip over.

Tried that cranberry-stringing thing, but the frozen cranberries mushed up when I defrosted them in the microwave. Oh, and here's a tip: Don't use those new chocolate-flavored Rice Krispies in that snowball recipe unless you're ready for some rather disgusting comments from your kids. I put a few too many marshmallows in mine, and they flattened out into disks I thought looked like hockey pucks—but the kids insisted were cow patties.

Gotta go. The smoke alarm is going off.

Love,<br>Erma

If you're not into making your own paper, mixing your own paint, firing your own pottery, or stringing your own cranberry garlands, hurray! It means you have more time to be silly and share your joy with others.

### Decorating Doozies

It's incredible to realize the effort some people will make to create something unique and memorable for their homes. A friend in Florida has an extraordinary forty-foot-tall artificial tree in the atrium of her magnificent house; the tree has twenty-five thousand silk leaves, and each one was carefully glued in place by the tree's creator.

Similar treasures are being created right now by many quilting enthusiasts who are finishing up "millennium quilts" to commemorate the turn of the century. Each quilt is comprised of two thousand tiny pieces carefully stitched together. Even more mind-boggling is the goal of some quilters to have two thousand pieces cut from two thousand different fabrics! Imagine!

And it's not just our private homes that are being decorated with such amazing features. Not too long ago I saw a newspaper picture showing a huge statue of Godzilla that adorned a Tokyo hotel lobby. The ten-foot-tall monster, created by the hotel's chefs, was made from fourteen thousand pieces of bread.

The designers of the display in the baggage-claim area of the Sacramento airport may have had the same idea of using common items to create "art." When we flew into Sacramento last year, I was stunned to see a huge stack of luggage near the carousel where our bags were to arrive. And then I noticed another huge stack—and another! They were all over the place!

And there, in the middle of one stack, was *my* suitcase. Or at least I thought it was until I walked over for a closer look. Then I discovered the suitcases—hundreds of old ones, new ones, suitcases of all colors and sizes—were stuck together, piled from floor to ceiling. Talk about ways to be creative with *clutter*! Either they were using the suitcases to hold up the roof—or it was supposed to be art!

## Simple Comforts

Thank heaven we *all* don't have to think up unusual ways to use stale bread and old luggage to make our homes appealing. In fact, the simplest things sometimes mean the most to guests and family members. For instance, I saw a newspaper article recently that said, "One of the greatest concerns of American families" is "running out of toilet paper."[2] Wow! How amazing to think that simply by keeping our bathrooms stocked with tissue we can wipe out all sorts of family anxieties. Not too long after that article appeared, someone sent me another item that said part of our laundry worries may be eliminated someday too. It reported that in an effort to find new ways to dispose of astronauts' dirty underwear, "Russian scientists are developing a strain of bacteria that will eat underpants."[3] Wouldn't that be wonderful?

In addition to pants-eating bacteria, all sorts of new ideas are in the works now to make homemaking and home decorating easier. For example, for those who love houseplants but can't manage to keep them alive (mine usually die in the backseat on the way home from the nursery), there's a new electronic "plant-sitter" designed to keep up to thirty plants alive. The thing costs $130 and resembles a giant squid; it might be easier to buy silk foliage.

Other technological doodads promise to make our homes intriguing, if not overwhelming, in the near future. For example, there's a new kitchen sink that comes complete with a heater underneath it, so you can cook things in it as well as clean up afterward![4] Somehow it doesn't sound all that appetizing to me, but then, nowadays all I do in the kitchen is dust, so it doesn't really matter.

Another wave of technology will have us *talking* to our alarm clocks at bedtime, telling them what to turn off, what to lock up, and under what conditions to awaken us the next morning ("If the traffic is heavy, get me up a half-hour early; if the dog's in the trash again, wake up Billy, no matter what time it is; if it snows, get Ted up so he can rev up the snowblower"). And those reminder notes we stick on our refrigerators? Someday, they'll appear as electronic marquees ("Janie, if it's four o'clock and you're reading this, you're in the wrong place—piano lesson, remember?"). That idea reminds me of the message one jokester left on his answering machine. It says, "Hi! John's answering machine is broken. This is his refrigerator. Please speak very slowly, and I'll stick your message to myself with one of these magnets."

In the future, it may even be possible to transfer phone messages to the bathroom mirror if we want. (Now, *that* would put me in a real bind, trying to decide whether I'd want to see my face at 6:00 A.M.—or a message reminding me of my pap-smear appointment.) Even our trash cans will be wired in the future. As we throw things away, they'll scan the trash and create a grocery list. And best of all, while we sleep, a quiet, sonar-guided robot vacuum cleaner will cruise through the house sucking up dog hair and Twinkie crumbs.[5]

"Hey, how about some volunteers to stay and help clean up?"

Now, while we're waiting for these space-age gizmos of the future to appear at Kmart, I'll help you pass the time by sharing two little tips for the here-and-now (just so you won't think I'm completely lost in the kitchen).

- Best Company Dessert to Serve When You Don't (or Won't) Cook: Individually wrapped ice cream bars served in an ice bucket with a big plate of cookies.[6]

- Best Way to Prevent Violence and Insanity When Trying to Find the End of the Plastic-Wrap Roll: Keep the wrap in your freezer. I don't know why it works, but it usually does.[7]

One of the easy and fun things we did to decorate when our boys were at home was to stick glow-in-the-dark stars on the ceilings of their rooms. They were barely noticeable during the day but at night emitted a soft, cheery glow. One of the first times Tim went to sleep over at a friend's house, he came home with a whole new appreciation for my decorating skills. He said, "Mom, I didn't like it over there. They didn't have any stars on the ceiling."

When we were in Memphis last year, we got a whole new perspective on home decor when our hostess took us to Graceland, Elvis Presley's estate. We had heard a lot about the outlandish decorating style "the king" had lavished on his home. And things *were* pretty amazing there. The "jungle room," for instance, not only had the green shag carpeting so many thousands of us covered our floors with in the 1970s, it also boasted a floor-to-ceiling stone *waterfall* and massive furniture upholstered with fake fur and supported by elaborately carved wooden arms and sides. Each piece looked as if it weighed a ton. The huge coffee table was made from a slice of a gigantic hardwood tree, and the gnarled base and edges were carved to make the table look as though it were a thousand years old.

The stairs leading to the basement were completely encased in mirrors, creating such an illusion of infinity that the guides warned people with vertigo and other vision and balance problems to skip that part of the tour. One basement room had three TV sets lined up beside each other on a counter. And the billiards room was swathed in nearly four hundred yards of cotton fabric bearing a busy geometric pattern that caused my astigmatism to flare up.

It was an incredible place. Many of the tourists seemed to scoff at the overdone decorating themes that grew increasingly unreal as we moved through the house, but the images that really stuck with us were created by the stories the tour guides told about the fun Elvis had enjoyed in those places. We heard about the rollicking, late-night jam sessions, the way Elvis and his daughter played in the snow, the jokes he liked to play on his friends. In the hall where his gold and platinum award records were displayed, we were told that he had sold enough records to circle the globe. But even more impressive to me was imagining "the king" sitting at the simple piano where he often played and sang beloved old gospel songs he'd learned as a boy.

As we left Elvis's mansion, our heads were buzzing with what we'd seen. But then for some reason I happened to remember a billboard back in California that advertised a local Christian bookstore. It says, "Graceland—where the KING *really* lives!" Elvis's mansion was really something, but Christians know who the *real* King is.

"Go get the phone number of those idiots who installed the vinyl siding."

## Decorating Our Lives

Just as we find ways to decorate our homes for personal comfort, we also decorate our lives for personal relationships. One woman wrote to tell me she had decorated her entire home with rainbows, the symbols of hope. Rainbows adorn her kitchen, bedrooms, doormats, suncatchers, stationery, bank checks, refrigerator magnets, and greeting cards, she said. And her life is decorated with hope.

Another letter-writer lost her home completely after a bitter divorce. Her daughter helped her get over it when she said, "That's OK, Mom. Jesus is working on your mansion right now."

What that daughter was saying was spelled out in another letter from a different mother. Her heart had been broken, and she had been through some extremely hard times. But she had a choice about where she was going to live now. "Thank you, Barbara," she wrote, "for showing me that I do have a choice—either to live in a pit or to climb out and open up my arms wide to God and let Him work through me."

It's a choice offered to each of us every day of our lives.

Our days are identical suitcases—all the same size—but some people can pack more into them than others.[8]

When I think of the unusual display of luggage at the airport in Sacramento, I love remembering the line from a friend's letter. She said my books were like "very large suitcases crammed full of good things, enduring things, fun things— and most of all . . . *HOPE!*" What a wonderful compliment!

An elderly carpenter was ready to retire after several decades of high-quality, dependable work for his contractor boss. He told his employer of his plans to leave the house-building business and enjoy a leisurely life with his wife and extended family. He would miss the paycheck, he said, but he needed to retire. They could get by.

The contractor was sorry to see his good worker go. He asked if the carpenter would build just one more house as a personal favor. The carpenter said yes. But as time went by it was easy to see that his heart was not in his work. He resorted to shoddy workmanship and used inferior materials, believing that, since it was his last house, it didn't matter if his reputation was maintained. He no longer cared.

When the carpenter finished his work, the contractor came to say good-bye. As he turned to go, the contractor handed the carpenter the key to the house he had just built. "This is your house," the boss said. "It is my gift to you."

If I live in a spotless mansion of pristine beauty with everything in its place . . .

If I have time to polish the windows, mop the floors, clean the bathroom floors—but have no time to show love . . .

If I train my children to cook and clean and mow and paint but do not teach them to love . . .

Then I am a housekeeper, not a mother; a manager, not a shepherd.

> No matter what I say, what I believe, and
> what I do, I'm bankrupt without love.
> Love never gives up.
> Love cares more for others than for self.
> Love doesn't want what it doesn't have.
> Love doesn't strut,
> Doesn't have a swelled head,
> Doesn't force itself on others,
> Isn't always "me first,"
> Doesn't fly off the handle,

Doesn't keep score of the sins of others,
Doesn't revel when others grovel,
Takes pleasure in the flowering of truth,
Puts up with anything,
Trusts God always,
Always looks for the best,
Never looks back,
But keeps going to the end.
Love never dies.[9]

**HERMAN®**

3-18     © Jim Unger/dist. by United Media, 1999

**"Look what your stupid uncle gave us.
What d'you think it is?"**

### Kitchen Rules

1. If a messy kitchen is a happy kitchen, my kitchen is delirious.
2. A husband is someone who takes out the trash and gives the impression he just cleaned the whole kitchen.
3. Countless people have eaten in this kitchen . . . and gone on to lead normal lives.

The nicest gift is always something you made yourself . . . like money.[10]

Did you hear about the doorbell and hummingbird who fell in love?
They had a little humdinger![11]

Sign posted at a retirement village:
"LORD, PLEASE KEEP ME ALIVE WHILE I'M STILL LIVING!"[12]

Riddle:
What's gray, crispy and hangs from the ceiling?
An amateur electrician.[13]

To live in hearts we leave behind . . . is not to die.

—THOMAS CAMPBELL

I've discovered an interesting phenomenon: If you keep microwaving bacon until it gets "real crispy" it will eventually melt down, and you will have to suck the flavor out of the paper towel. Amazing!

Bill says, "Barb cooks for fun, but for *food* we go out."

I can't cook, hate to clean, and loathe ironing. The only thing domestic about me is that I was born in this country.[14]

What if God had an answering machine?

"Hello, thank you for calling heaven. Please select one of the following four options: Press 1 for requests, 2 for thanksgiving, 3 to complain, or 4 for all other inquiries."

No matter what you press, you hear, "All angels are helping other members of God's family right now. Please stay on the line, and your call will be answered in the order it was received."

"To find out how many angels dance on the head of a pin, press 5.

"If you would like King David to sing a psalm for you, press 6.

"To find out if your relative is here, enter his or her date of death and then listen to the list that follows.

"To confirm your reservation, press the letters J-O-H-N and the numbers 3-1-6.

*Thank goodness we have God's promise that He is THE Operator who is standing by.*

Then you will call out, and the LORD will answer. You will cry out, and he will say, "Here I am."

—ISAIAH 58:9 NCV

# If They Can Send a Man to the Moon...
# Why Can't They Send 'Em All?

### Marriage Is a Great Institution. That's Why So Many Women End Up Institutionalized

One morning last summer when Bill was out of town I happened to be standing in the driveway when my neighbor drove by. She rolled down the window, gestured toward the pile of trash I'd put out for the garbage truck, and said sadly, "We can sure tell when Bill's not here!"

*Well, you don't have to rub it in!* I thought as I surveyed the untidy heap of trash bags, boxes, and newspapers I'd managed to drag out to the curb. It *did* look different from the neat, perfectly symmetrical, snowball-shaped bags that Bill usually leaves out for the trash truck. He not only flattens all the boxes, he also cuts up the milk cartons so the pieces can be stacked in neat blocks, which he binds with string before depositing them in the trash bag. He even rinses out the bottles and cans so there's no odor or stickiness. If there's one thing Bill takes pride in, it's his trash!

In contrast, I feel good if something I toss toward the trash can actually lands inside the bin. For me, life is too short to worry whether my garbage has curbside appeal. But such things are important to Bill. And when he was gone for those few days last year, I developed a new appreciation for several of his organizational eccentricities.

# HERMAN®

4-1    © Jim Unger/dist. by United Media, 1999

**"And another thing! I'm getting sick of you being so agreeable all the time."**

He's always traveled with me for my speaking appearances around the country, and he's always been the one who makes sure the room key is handy. (Now that hotel "keys" are like credit cards, they're so easy to lose and so hard to find!) When he stays behind in the hotel room while I'm out running errands or attending meetings, he leaves the door ajar so I can get back in without digging through my purse for the key. Those things hadn't meant much to me until I had to travel alone last year while he was away.

At the hotel, for the first time in my memory (which, granted, isn't all that sharp these days, but it still seemed so strange) I had to figure out which way to slide the key into the mechanism to unlock the door to my room. Then, when I got inside, I looked around, wondering where my luggage was.

You see, when we arrive at a hotel, I usually go straight to the front desk to check in while Bill oversees the luggage handling. I was embarrassed that day to realize my suitcases were still waiting in the circle drive where the limo driver had unloaded them. As soon as the limo stopped, I had hurried off to the front desk without giving them a second thought!

The time during that trip when I missed Bill the most, however, was at bedtime. Not because of any romantic moods or lonesome thoughts—although I did miss him. No, the thing I missed was having him there to set the hotel alarm clock. Although I called the hotel operator to arrange a wake-up call, we've found that service notoriously undependable, so Bill always sets the alarm clock too. When I traveled without him on that trip, he was so sure that I, being technologically challenged, wouldn't know how to set the alarm that he called me himself at 4:00 A.M. California time to make sure I was awake at 7:00 A.M. in Detroit!

Another thing about traveling alone that made me miss Bill was the clutter in the hotel bathroom. Now, Bill never clutters anything; usually the bathroom is completely filled with all my makeup, cleansing creams, shower caps, robe, and all those other essentials we women have to travel with. The thing I missed seeing was that one little spot on the bathroom countertop where Bill would leave his neatly zippered toiletries bag. It always seems like an island of peace in a sea of chaos, and when it wasn't there, I missed it.

It does seem that the bathroom is the place where differences between men and women are most noticeable, doesn't it? Someone sent me a little quip that said a typical man has six items in his bathroom: a toothbrush, toothpaste, shaving cream, razor, soap, and a towel. The typical woman, on the other hand, has an average of 437 items in her bathroom—and most men are unable to identify 431 of them!

One of the biggest bathroom controversies, of course, is how to get men to put the seat down on the commode. Recently I was interested to see that someone in England had devised a gadget that automatically lowers the seat after the

**Blondie**

toilet is flushed. There are rumors that the inventor is being nominated for the Nobel Peace Prize.

Husbands and wives often learn to deal with their differences as they gain greater intimacy. This funny story by an unknown writer shows just how intimate some couples can get:

A young man noticed that an elderly couple sitting down to lunch at McDonald's had ordered just one meal and an extra drink cup. As he watched, the gentleman carefully divided the hamburger in half then counted out the fries, one for him, one for her, until each had half of them. Next he poured half of the soft drink into the extra cup and set that in front of his wife. The old man then began to eat, and his wife sat watching, her hands folded demurely in her lap.

The young man decided to ask if they would allow him to purchase another meal for them so they didn't have to split theirs.

"Oh, no," the old gentleman replied. "We've been married fifty years, and everything has always been and will always be shared, fifty-fifty."

The young man then asked the wife if she was going to eat.

"Not yet," she replied. "It's his turn with the teeth."

That story always reminds me of the time Bill went down to In 'n' Out Hamburgers, just a block away, to pick up a little treat for us. When he got there, he ordered two hamburgers and two orders of french fries. But when he got the bag home, he started spreading it out and found only one hamburger and one order of fries.

"Oh," he said to me. "That's too bad. I guess they must have forgotten yours!"

**Beetle Bailey**

Reprinted with special permission of King Features Syndicate.

## Men Are Funny

Let's face it. When men aren't making us pull our hair out, they're often making us laugh. Another story by an unknown writer described how a man with his arm in a cast could not give a convincing explanation of how he had broken his arm. He finally confessed that it had happened when his wife brought some potted plants indoors after they had been out on the patio all day. A friendly garter snake had hidden in one of the pots, and later when it slithered out across the floor the wife spotted it.

"I was in the bathtub when I heard her scream wildly," he related. "I thought she was being murdered, so I jumped out of the tub and ran to help her. I didn't even grab a towel. When I ran into the living room, she yelled that a snake was under the couch. I got down on all fours to look for it, and just then my dog came up from behind and 'cold-nosed' me. I guess I thought it was the snake, and I fainted dead away. My wife thought I'd had a heart attack and called for an ambulance. I was still groggy when the paramedics arrived. They lifted me onto a stretcher, and just as they were carrying me out, the snake came out from under the couch and obviously frightened one of the paramedics. He dropped his end of the stretcher—and that's how I broke my arm."

Men hate to admit they'd get caught in such silly scenarios. But someone out there has to do stupid things if for no other reason than to keep the rest of us entertained! Apparently, improbable acts of foolishness are more common than you would think. An article in *Newsweek* last spring listed some warnings that now appear on everyday products—apparently because enough folks have somehow used those things to hurt themselves in unimaginable ways. For example:

- On bread pudding: "Product will be hot after heating."

- On a bar of soap: "Use like regular soap."

- On a hotel shower cap: "Fits one head."

- On a package of sleeping pills: "May cause drowsiness."

- On a string of Christmas lights: "For indoor or outdoor use only."

- And best of all, this warning appeared on an iron: "Do not iron clothes on body."[1]

Now, I could be wrong about this, but somehow I just can't quite picture a woman trying to iron a blouse while she's wearing it. No, the image that comes to mind is more likely to be a man, lying down on the floor, trying to iron a crease in the legs of his trousers. Which brings to mind another ridiculous story someone sent me. It describes how a young man happened to show up at a family reunion with extremely red ears—*burned* ears, actually. In all seriousness, the man explained that it had been a long, lazy weekend afternoon when he had flipped mindlessly from one football game to another. His wife was ironing in the same room, and she had set the phone on the ironing board so she could talk to her mother while she worked.

She had left the room to carry the ironed clothes to the bedroom when suddenly the phone rang.

"I was deeply engrossed in the game at that point," the young man said. "So, keeping my eyes glued to the television, I grabbed the hot iron and put it to my ear, thinking it was the telephone."

"But how did *both* ears get burned?" someone asked.

"I hadn't any more than hung up," the man said, "when the guy called back!"

"No, dear. The phone's working fine — you just answered the TV remote."

Having to admit they are capable of doing stupid things isn't the only thing that's embarrassing for some men. One of the scariest things some of them do is accompany their wives to the mall, especially at Christmastime, when the traffic is hectic and the stores are packed. One researcher said the stress levels in some men skyrocket when they're faced with crowded stores. The scientist compared it with the heart rate and blood pressure "you would expect to find in a 'fighter pilot going into combat.'"[2]

Knowing how stressful it can be for him, I insist on driving when Bill accompanies me to the mall. I've adapted a strategic plan someone suggested for finding a parking space. What you do is hang your head out the car window . . . be very quiet . . . and listen for a motor to turn over. Then you tear across the parking lot in the direction of the sound, driving *against* the arrows, to try to get to that space first. Other than someone dying and leaving you a parking spot, I don't know of any other way to get one during the holiday rush.

**NON SEQUITUR**

Besides shopping, there are other things that may cause men's stress levels to rise. One stressful activity is brushing their hair and finding that they're becoming, shall we say, *folicularly challenged*. This is a devastating loss for many men. It reminds me of the quip that claims Adam was the luckiest man ever to live, in part because "if he had gone bald, no one would have known that wasn't normal."

Men may get all sorts of crazy ideas when their hair falls outs, and commercial organizations have no shame in promoting an endless variety of products aimed at camouflaging the loss. One of the more creative products combines particles

of Australian sheep wool with an adhesive spray that (along
with static electricity) holds them in place. One newspaper
reporter described it this way:

> The stuff comes in a can that looks like a pepper shaker.
> You sprinkle the fibers on your head, trying not to pre-
> tend you're a pot roast, then pat your hair, apply a little
> Fiberhold Spray and off you go. Ta da.[3]

No sensitive woman would ever mention such a touchy
subject to her husband. Experienced wives know there are
certain topics that just shouldn't be brought up. The topics to
be avoided depend on each couple's issues, of course. In a
magazine article last year a political wife told how she'd
learned to refrain from criticizing one important topic: her
husband's speeches. She said that after she'd criticized one of
her husband's speeches, "he came home for weeks afterward
with [supporters'] letters saying it was his *best* speech ever."

Then, one night, as the politician and his wife were pulling
into the driveway, he said to her, "Tell me the truth. How *was*
that speech?"

She told him quietly, "It wasn't that good"—and her husband "drove right into the garage wall."[4]

**The Lockhorns**

"We can't agree on a long-distance provider."

And then there's the issue of how men so often refuse to stop for *anything* once they've begun any kind of trip. Have you heard the joke about what would have happened if there had been three wise *women* instead of wise *men*? They would have stopped to ask for directions, arrived on time, helped deliver the baby, cleaned up the stable, made a casserole, and brought disposable diapers and other *practical* gifts!

Along those same lines, someone came up with this goofy list of how things would be different if *men* got pregnant:

• Maternity leave would last two years—with full pay.

• There'd be a cure for stretch marks.

• Natural childbirth would become obsolete.

• Morning sickness would rank as the nation's number one health problem.

• Children would be kept in the hospital until they were potty trained.

• Men could use *their* briefcases as diaper bags.

• Paternity suits would be a line of clothing.

• They'd stay in bed for the entire nine months.

### Love, Laughter, and Togetherness

With all these differences existing between millions of husbands and wives, it's a wonder the "institution" of marriage survives at all. As Bill Cosby said, "That married couples can live together day after day is a miracle the Vatican has overlooked." One reason it continues, say researchers, is simply because . . . it works. Marriage is "a glorious mess," one writer said. It "is pretty good for the goose much of the time, but golden for the gander practically all of the time." In other words, "Marriage has a beneficial effect for both men and women, but the effect is much stronger for men. . . . They may resist, they may kick and scream about getting married, but then it does them a world of good." Other studies show that "matrimony adds more years to a man's life than it does to a woman's. . . . Marriage can even make frail men strong," researchers say.[5]

It makes sense, then, that losing a spouse "hits men harder than it does women."[6]

Perhaps that explains what happened last year when I opened an envelope that came in the mail to find a check made out to me and signed by a man. Most noticeably, at the bottom of the check the man had written, "DO NOT SELL OUR NAME TO ANY MAILING LISTS! DO NOT SEND SOLICITATIONS OR MATERIALS! DO NOT CONTACT US!"

Flabbergasted to get such a note, I noticed the phone number was printed on the check, and I decided I'd call the guy up and ask why he would write such a message!

In a cold, gruff tone, he told me his wife had attended a recent Women of Faith conference. He hadn't wanted her to go, he said, because she was in very poor health. In fact, in December her doctor had given her less than three months to live. Then, in January, some friends bundled her up in a wheelchair and took her to the conference.

"Well . . . what happened?" I asked fearfully.

"Oh, she loved it," he said, his tone warming slightly. "She came home bubbling over with all the stuff she'd seen and heard. And she asked me to send you that check to pay for books she'd gotten from your book table. She hadn't taken her checkbook and didn't have enough cash after lunch, and one of the helpers at your book table gave her the books and said she could send the money later. So she asked me to write the check. But I've heard about these Christian organizations that are always after you for money once they get your name on their mailing lists. And I don't want any part of that."

I assured him we weren't about to sell or use his name on *any* mailing lists. "Why, I've got three shoeboxes full of names of people who *want* to be on our mailing list and we can't get them on. I'm not about to add someone who doesn't want to be on it." I also gave him the address of the bulk-mail organization he could register with to get his name off junk-mail lists. (It doesn't work, but I thought giving it to him might calm him down.)

Finally, I got up the nerve to ask, "Well, how is your wife now?"

"She's here. Would you like to speak to her?" he asked.

"Oh, I'd love to speak to her!" I answered.

The man obviously left the room. I think he was embarrassed—and he should have been!

When the woman got to the phone, she said, "Oh, Barbara! I can't believe you called! Thank you so much for those books. I've already read them, and I just loved them."

She said she thought the conference was wonderful, and she remembered that I had talked about a new book I was doing about heaven called *He's Gonna Toot, and I'm Gonna Scoot.* "Oh, Barb, I'd love to read it . . . but you said it'll be three months before the book is out, and by then . . . I'll be gone."

"Yeah, you'll be gone," I agreed sadly before I realized what I was saying.

Then I had an idea: "Well, I have a rough copy of the manuscript, and I'd be glad to send it to you—to *you*, not to *him!*"

She said, "Oh, I'd just love that!"

So I sent the manuscript to her—to *her*, not to *him!*—and in a couple of days she called and said, "Barb, I'm just so happy to have that manuscript. It's going to be a wonderful book. But now I have a favor to ask of you—would you do it?"

I said, "Oh, Honey! I'd do anything for you!"

She paused a moment then said, "Well, when I'm gone, my husband is going to be so desolate and so alone. . . . Would you mind putting him on your mailing list to get your newsletter?"

Even though we poke fun at our husbands and their different way of doing things, most of us have chosen to link our lives with theirs and face whatever comes, good or bad, laughter or tears. As Thomas Merton said:

Even saints cannot live with saints on this earth without some anguish, without some pain at the differences that come between them. . . . Love is the resetting of a body of broken bones.

**Murray's Law by Leslie Moak Murray**

The happiest marriages are surely those where love and laughter overcome any brokenness. Between these couples, laughter is a natural part of every day. One friend sent me a packet of funny poems and stories she wanted to share. She had hoped to also send a photocopy of her favorite cartoon, titled "The Incurable Romantic." But she couldn't copy it, because her husband had *glued* it inside the door of their medicine cabinet! Instead she had to tell me what it said. The illustration, she said, showed a man climbing into bed with his wife, and saying, "The light reflected off your night cream is like moonlight on a still mountain pool, and the silver gleam of curlers under the hair net suggests dew on cobwebs in some remote glade."

Can't you just see that husband and wife, chuckling every morning when they open the medicine cabinet to reach for the toothpaste?

Other husbands may lack this guy's sense of humor but find other ways to keep a marriage alive. One woman, who fought major depression after learning her son was a homosexual, wrote to say,

There was a time when I was so sad all the time, but I can now experience joy in life in many areas. My husband gave me a wake-up call when I was so blue. He looked at me with tears in his eyes and said, "You still have *me*." That was a turning point for me. I cannot let this problem destroy my life and those around me.

This kind of "we're-in-it-together" attitude of another husband and wife was honored last year when a *Washington Post* columnist wrote about ninety-six-year-old Mike Mansfield, the former U.S. Senate majority leader. After lying about his age and joining the navy at age fourteen, Mansfield went to Montana to work in the copper mines. There he "met a young schoolteacher who recognized his exceptional qualities and encouraged him to pursue an education. After sixty-eight years of marriage to Maureen Hayes, the teacher, his devotion is undiminished."

My favorite part of the story came in the next sentence, which noted that "the Montana Legislature recently proposed erecting a statue of Mansfield in the state capitol in Helena." Mansfield's reply to the legislature was easy: "If it's just me, no; if it's Maureen and me, OK."[7]

**"What I said was, 'I'm feeling *rheumatic!*'"**

Another illustration of this kind of togetherness exists on Vashon Island, Washington, just south of Seattle. There a living phenomenon is becoming something of an attraction. It is the Bicycle Tree, a bit of "magic," according to writer Charis Collins, "that began when a young child leaned a little red bicycle into the tree's young, reaching crook and never returned for it. As the tree matured, it embraced the bicycle without complaint, drawing the tiny handlebars, the banana seat, the rotted tires to itself most naturally. . . . The two have become intertwined inexplicably, forever unable to separate. These days the tree literally has grown into the bicycle, and the bicycle has stretched with it, curiously raised several feet off the ground, encased lovingly by the tender, knotty trunk."

To Charis, the Bicycle Tree reminds her "of how Grandpa and Grandma's wedding rings look to me, embedded in the creases of their thick, worn fingers." It also symbolizes how she sees their marriage:

> Marriage is taking on another person in life. It is not usually planned from the beginning; you don't know who it will be when you are born . . . , but somehow the two joined become one, even if it doesn't seem likely or at all possible. If you are lucky, you grow more entangled with each passing day.[8]

*Entangled* is the perfect word for couples tied to each other by the bonds of matrimony. Sometimes we're wound up and crisscrossed like contestants playing the old Twister game. And other times, it feels as if we're irreparably stuck in one big knot. But without that tangled knot, I know for sure I'd be at loose ends, because there's a third strand running through our marriage that ties us, not only to each other, but also to our Creator. That strand is God's love for us.

> If two lie down together, they will keep warm. But how can one keep warm alone? . . . A cord of three strands is not quickly broken. (Eccles. 4:11–12)

## Squirts & Squints

**This is a rule for women that has no exceptions:**
If it has tires or testosterone, you're gonna have trouble with it.

Two small cousins were straining to hear what was going on at a recent wedding. The older cousin turned to her father and asked, "Dad, what are they saying?"

"They're saying their vows," the father whispered.

The girl turned and dutifully passed on the news to her cousin: "They're saying their A-E-I-O-U's," she carefully explained.[9]

*Veni, vedi, visa*
Translation: I came, I saw, I did a little shopping.

I have a little red box with a little red button on it. If someone asks me what it's for, I have to tell them, "Whenever I push that button, absolutely nothing happens. It just keeps me humble!"

If men can run the world, why can't they stop wearing neckties? How intelligent is it to start the day by tying a little noose around your neck?

—LINDA ELLERBEE

A good way to have the last word . . .
is to apologize.

Dear Lord, prop us up in all our leaning ways.

Engraved on the tombstone of the mother of nine children:
Here Lies Mom.
Let Her R.I.P.

Wise husbands know that PMS is Mother Nature's way of saying, "Get out of the house!"

Somewhere between ice cream and being buried alive.... is........

P.M.S.

© David Horrocks, Muskrat Springs, Inc. Used by permission.

One Sunday a pastor told his congregation the church needed some extra money. He asked the people to prayerfully consider giving a little extra in the offering plate. He said that whoever gave the most would be allowed to pick out three hymns.

The offering plates were passed, and the pastor was delighted to find a check for a thousand dollars. He announced the "winner," and a quiet, elderly, saintly lady shyly made her way to the front of the church. The pastor told her how wonderful it was that she had given so much. In thanksgiving, he asked her to pick out three hymns.

Her eyes brightened as she looked over the congregation, pointed to the three handsomest men in the building, and said, "I'll take him, him, and him!"

**A joke:**
Do old men wear boxers or briefs?
*Depends!*

**Bumper Sticker:**
Few women admit their age.
Fewer men act it.

Man trying to meet woman: "Hey, sweetie, what's your sign?"
Woman: "Do Not Enter."

A man was walking along a California beach and stumbled across an old lamp.

He picked it up and rubbed it, and out popped a genie. The

genie said, "OK, OK. You released me from the lamp. This is the fourth time this month, and I'm getting tired of these wishes, so you can forget about getting three. You only get one wish! What is it?"

The man thought about it awhile and said, "I've always wanted to go to Hawaii, but I'm afraid to fly and I get very seasick. Could you build a bridge to Hawaii so I can drive over there?"

The genie laughed and said, "Are you crazy? That's impossible! Think of the logistics of building a bridge like that! How would the supports ever reach the bottom of the Pacific? Think of how much steel I'd need! No. Think of something else."

The man said OK and tried to think of a really good wish.

Finally, he said, "I wish I could understand women—know how they feel and what they are thinking, understand why they cry and what makes them laugh. I want to know what they really want when they say 'nothing' and how to make them truly happy."

The genie paused a moment then answered, "Do you want that bridge two lanes or four?"

Within this grave we lie,
Back to back, my wife and I.
When the last trump the air shall fill
If she gets up, I'll just lie still.

—FEARFUL HUSBAND

I wonder . . .
What hair color do they put on the driver's licenses of bald men?

There are two theories for arguing with a woman.
Neither one works.

If women ran the world . . .

  The hem of men's pants would go up or down depending
  on the economy.

  Men who designed women's shoes would be forced to
  wear them.

  Men would bring drinks, chips, and dip to women
  watching soap operas.

  Men would sit around and wonder what *we're* thinking.

  All toilet seats would be nailed down.

### A Male-Designed Curriculum
### for Training Wives

1.  *Silence, the Final Frontier:* Where No Woman Has
    Gone Before
2.  *The Undiscovered Side of Banking:* Making Deposits
3.  *Man Management:* Postponing Minor Household
    Chores 'Til After the Game
4.  *Bathroom Etiquette I:* Men Need Medicine Cabinet
    Space Too
5.  *Bathroom Etiquette II:* His Razor Is His
6.  *Communication Skills I:* Tears—the Last Resort, Not
    the First
7.  *Communication Skills II:* Thinking Before Speaking
8.  *Communication Skills III:* Getting What You Want
    Without Nagging
9.  *Driving a Car Safely:* Introduction to Parking
10. *Telephone Skills 101:* How to Hang Up
11. *Water Retention:* Fact or Fat?
12. *Cooking I:* Bringing Back Bacon, Eggs, and Butter
13. *Advanced Cooking:* How Not to Inflict Your Diet on
    Other People
14. *PMS:* Your Problem . . . Not His
15. *Classic Clothing:* Wearing Outfits You Already Own
16. *Household Dust:* A Harmless Natural Occurrence Only
    Women Notice

17. *Integrating Your Laundry:* Washing It All Together
18. *Oil and Gas:* Your Car Needs *Both*
19. *TV Remotes:* For Men Only
20. *Shortening Your Attention Span:* How to Watch Fourteen TV Shows Simultaneously

Tell a man there are four hundred billion stars, and he'll believe you. Tell him a bench has wet paint, and he has to touch it.

—STEVEN WRIGHT

Only two things are necessary to keep one's wife happy. One is to let her think she is having her own way. The other is to let her have it.

—LYNDON B. JOHNSON

**DENNIS the MENACE**

"MY DAD'S A GOOD DRIVER BECAUSE MY MOM COACHES HIM."

Man is incomplete until he is married.
Then he's finished!

A little boy asked his father, "Daddy, how much does it cost to get married?"

The father replied, "I don't know, son. I'm still paying."

A woman marries a man expecting he will change, but he doesn't. A man marries a woman expecting that she won't change, and she does.

Ah, children! A woman knows all about her children. She knows about dentist appointments and soccer games and romances and best friends and favorite foods and secret fears and hopes and dreams.

A man is vaguely aware of some short people living in the house.

A little girl was having a hard time grasping the concept of marriage. In an attempt to help, her father got out the wedding album and explained the ceremony to her.

"Oh, I see," the little girl said. "That's when Mommy came to work for us!"

My dear brothers and sisters, always be willing to listen and slow to speak. Do not become angry easily, because anger will not help you live the right kind of life God wants. . . . In gentleness accept God's teaching that is planted in your hearts, which can save you. (James 1:19–21 NCV)

# When Your Road Is All Downhill . . .
## You're Probably Holding
## the Map Upside Down

*God grant me the senility to forget the
people I never liked anyway, the good
fortune to run into the ones I do—and the
eyesight to know the difference.*

**S**ometime back Bill and I were going to a retreat in Texas,
and the dear gals who were to pick us up at the airport in
Houston were overwhelmed by their assigned jobs and nervous about making sure everything would go perfectly.
Unfortunately, almost nothing did!

The first mix-up occurred when they mistakenly thought we
were flying into Houston's smaller Hobby Airport. Instead, we
landed at the much larger Intercontinental. (It's so big some frequent flyers have nicknamed it Houston Intergalactic Airport.)
Then, when they discovered their first mistake and arrived at
the right airport, they looked at our itinerary and saw that we
were flying in from Ontario—and assumed that meant we were
arriving from Canada at the international terminal. Instead, we
were really flying from Ontario, California!

As a result, Bill and I waited in the luggage area for an hour with no one showing up. Then, far down the corridor, we spotted two figures rushing toward us. I knew they were coming for *us*, because as they trotted down the concourse they were struggling to control huge, sombrero-sized hats with geraniums flying off them in every direction. They rushed up to us, apologizing in their charming southern accents for being so late and explaining about going to the wrong airport and then the wrong terminal in the right airport. Finally they hustled us out to the one lady's lovely new Town Car, piled our luggage in the trunk, and headed out of the parking lot on the two-hour trip to the little town about eighty miles away where the retreat was to be held.

The disaster continued.

The two hostesses, still wearing their huge hats, sat in front so Bill and I could feel as if we were being chauffeured. As we pulled out of the parking lot, the driver confessed, from beneath her sombrero, "Barb, I have NO idea where this retreat is, and I've never driven around this airport before, so I have to call my husband for directions." She explained that she would *never* have agreed to be our driver if she'd known we were flying into *this* airport instead of her familiar Hobby.

It turned out her husband was a judge in a Houston court, and she called him on her cellular phone while we drove rather aimlessly around the airport freeway system. She didn't have a pen and paper—and even if she had, of course, she couldn't write, drive, and talk on the cell phone, so I sat in the backseat, trying to interpret her deep southern drawl and write down the directions she relayed from the judge. He was quite patient but apparently realized he wasn't making any headway in relaying the directions. He directed her to pull out a map.

Her seatmate fumbled in the glove compartment, found a map, and spread it out over her lap. The driver continued relaying the judge's information to both of us, but the gal reading the map interrupted to say, "I can't find where we are or any of the roads he's describing!"

At that point, Bill, the former Eagle Scout whose motto is "Be Prepared," came to the rescue. He leaned over the seat, raised the rim of the second lady's sombrero to glance at the map, and said, "That's Mexico you're looking at. Why don't you turn it over and see if it might have Texas on the other side?"

"Oh, silly me!" giggled the navigator. She wrestled the map over to its other side and once again searched diligently for something that sounded familiar. But the printing was so small she gave up, admitting she still couldn't find anything. Once again Bill came to the rescue. He pulled out the magnifier he carries in his pocket and shoved it under the lady's hat. She took it from him with a puzzled tilt of her head and laid it down flat on the map. "Oh dear, it doesn't seem to help any, Bill," she commented, still confused.

"Lift it up!" Bill ordered.

The woman raised the magnifier a few inches from the map and exclaimed, "Oh, the words get *bigger* when you do that!"

Eventually we arrived at the little town (proving once again that God *does* answer prayer!), and the retreat was bunches of fun. But I think Bill and I have had *more* fun recalling that hilarious encounter with those two charming but confused ladies (now that it's *over!*). As we watched them fumble through one goofy mix-up after another, I was sure we were observing some classic "senior moments." And we just love seeing senior moments in folks who are obviously younger than we are! Maybe we should just remember those gals as "geographically challenged" or "hormonally oversaturated," but "chronologically advanced" is my preferred excuse.

### Menopausal Moments

My friends love to tell me about their own menopausal moments when they do the silliest things. When one gal in her late forties was just tiptoeing into that hormonal cesspool, she had to drive her daughter to soccer practice several times a week. One of the intersections on the way to the soccer field was filled with fast-food places lined up next to each other, and the woman often stopped by the Burger King drive-through for her favorite sandwich after she dropped off her daughter.

One evening the drive-through was packed with a long line of cars, so the woman had to change her routine. Hurrying, she drove around the confusing collection of parking lots until she finally found a place to park and hustled inside to order.

Already frustrated by the delay and thinking about her tight schedule and many errands left to run, she was a bit crabby when she got to the cash register. A nervous-looking teenager stood behind the counter, expectantly waiting. Beside him towered the manager, trying to monitor the kid's work as he also yelled orders into the kitchen. *Great*, the woman thought. *I'm already in a hurry, and now I have to deal with a trainee.*

"I'd like a BK Broiler, no mayo, and a large Diet Coke," she ordered in her most no-nonsense tone.

The kid dropped his head and searched the cash register keyboard, obviously looking for the right button. His eyes moved left, right, up, down—and then back to the woman. "I'm sorry?" he asked.

"A BK Broiler . . . no mayo . . . and a large Diet Coke," the woman said deliberately and loudly, as though the kid had a hearing problem.

Once again the poor trainee searched the keyboard. By now completely flustered, he turned helplessly to the distracted manager while the woman rolled her eyes impatiently. The manager asked her to repeat the order one more time.

By now totally exasperated, the woman turned up the volume and enunciated slowly, "BK BROILER, NO MAYO, AND A LARGE DIET COKE!"

The manager paused only half a second before he replied deliberately, as though the woman had a mental problem, "MA'AM, THIS IS TACO BELL."

And then there was this funny story someone passed along about a sweet little lady who was well along the path to confusion corner:

Lola and Ned sat at the same bingo table and often walked home together. They took the shortcut through the adjacent cemetery.

One night Ned left early, so Lola had to walk home alone. Halfway through the cemetery she heard a faint noise—a voice calling, "Help, help." As Lola approached an open grave site, the voice was stronger. She peered down into the grave, and there lay Ned.

"Help me," he said. "I'm freezing."

Lola had a puzzled look on her face as she said to herself, *Ned is dead? I must have forgotten.* She said, "Of course I'll help you, Ned. You stay quiet while I get someone. No wonder you're cold. You've kicked off all your dirt."[1]

**DENNIS the MENACE**

"BOY! DAYS LIKE THIS MAKE ME FEEL YOUNG AGAIN!"

### I'm Only Old on the *Outside*

It's fun to laugh at these silly senior moments—as long as the stories aren't about us! We want to believe that no matter how old and shriveled we get on the outside, our brains are still humming along like a fine-tuned engine inside. If only we could get everyone to believe us when we protest that it's not our fault when we end up in ridiculous circumstances. That was the case when two longtime schoolteachers visited a drive-through wildlife park recently to check it out and see if it might be appropriate for their third-grade classes to visit on a field trip. If you've been to one of those parks, you know you're told to keep your windows rolled up, drive slowly, and be prepared to stop your vehicle to let the animals cross the road.

That's exactly what these two smart gals did. They stopped, spellbound, as an enormous elephant strolled across the road in front of them. But the beast didn't just cross the road. It stopped, its huge body completely blocking the two ladies' view out the windshield. And then a horrible thing happened. The elephant turned around, paused a moment, then *sat down* on the hood of their car! Hearing the car's metal groan and then crease pitifully under the weight, the two ladies were horrified, and for a moment they wondered if they were about to be crushed too. But the elephant apparently found the spot too uncomfortable and within a few seconds, it got up and ambled away, leaving in its dust the shocked women—and their smashed-in car.

Luckily, the car was still drivable, and the two schoolteachers hurried out of the park. They stopped to survey the damage at the first place down the road—a restaurant. They were far too upset to eat anything, but they went inside to try to calm down. Neither woman ever drank alcohol, but they decided that just this once, a glass of wine might be a good idea.

Eventually they finished the wine and got back into the crumpled car to drive home. By this time it was dark, and they'd gone only a few miles when a policeman stopped them because their headlights were cattywampus. One was pointing skyward while the other dangled morosely out of its socket. When the driver rolled down her window, the policeman smelled wine on her breath and ordered her out of the car.

At that point, the story came pouring out of the ladies, and the two schoolteachers begged the policeman not to arrest them. They pointed to the third-grade textbooks and teaching materials in the backseat, showed him their ticket stubs to the animal park, and assured him they were telling the truth. He listened to them with amused disbelief then stood quietly surveying the scene for a moment while the ladies held their wine-ladened breaths, knowing he held their fate in his hands. In a moment he snapped the ticket book closed and told the women they could leave.

"You're not gonna give me a ticket?" the driver anxiously asked.

"Ma'am, if I put this story in my report, I'd be laughed off the police force," he said. "Please stay out of the wildlife park in the future. OK?"

Can't you just see these prim and proper schoolteachers trying to explain their fender bender—and blaming an elephant?

## Age Is Important—If You're Cheese

After reading about a recent Harvard University study, I'm starting to wonder if my fondness for funny stories may be a double-edged sword. The study looked for similarities among those who live to be very old—in fact, older than one

hundred. One of the threads they found running through these "centenarian personalities" was that most of these folks who lived to be one hundred years old or older were "generally optimistic and, in most cases, funny. They use humor all the time," one of the researchers said.[2]

The report is a Catch-22 for me, because I love to laugh, but I'm also eagerly awaiting the sound of that celestial trumpet that will summon me to heaven! I'm not sure I *want* to live to be one hundred—and a lot of other people apparently feel the same way. Another recent survey reported, "The once-elusive goal of turning 100 years old is becoming more attainable every day. But a majority of Americans don't want to live that long."[3]

After all, by the time we've lived to be one hundred years old, our hearts will have beaten 3,681,619,200 times, pumping 27,323,260 gallons of blood weighing more than one hundred tons! Just thinking about it exhausts me. Even more amazing was the news story that said centenarians comprise the fastest-growing segment of the American population. And, the article adds, women in that age group outnumber men five to one![4]

But so far, old age just seems to be the direction I'm headed. Sometimes I feel like the fellow who was asked how he managed to live so long. He shrugged and replied simply, "I didn't die."

**Making Each Day Matter**
As long as I'm not dying, I'd like to do something productive—or at least something that makes me laugh. My mail is full of clippings friends have sent to me that describe others who share my love of life and laughter, no matter how old they are. Here's a sample:

- A ninety-eight-year-old Florida woman who goes ballroom dancing twice a week. (Her motto is, "Smile awhile, and while you smile another smiles, and soon there's miles and miles of smiles, and life's worthwhile because you smiled.")[5]

- A seventy-two-year-old Colorado runner who has been running—and winning—a ten-kilometer race at high altitude for the last seventeen years. Last year her goal was to finish in less than an hour.[6]

- A ninety-three-year-old Texas woman who recently helped paint a historical mural in her town.[7]

- A 108-year-old woman in Florida who learned to play the piano and organ at age seventy, rode a camel and hiked through Israel at age ninety-nine, and, last we heard, was enjoying reading e-mail notes sent to her web page on the Internet.[8]

- Two New York women who wrote their first book, a bestseller, *after* they were one hundred years old.[9]

- A Georgia woman who, at 101, is the oldest practicing physician in the United States.[10]

"It's not fair. Just as I'm turning into my mother,
she gets to turn into a grandma."

### Riding the Hormonal Hurricane

We gals have an extra road bump to deal with on our way to the golden years—menopause. We blame this hormonal hurricane for all sorts of maladies that range from hot flashes and forgetfulness to weight gain and tearfulness. How nice it is to know there are women out there who are actually celebrating this zany stage of life. In fact, 52 percent of American women between ages forty-five and sixty told a recent survey that "they consider menopause the beginning of a new and fulfilling stage."[11] *Those* are the gals *I* want to sit next to in the geriatric doctor's waiting room!

One of those optimistic gals was surely the sweet lady who gave me an adorable little doll called the Estrogen Fairy. The doll is a soft, tubby, little white-haired figure who sports a superhero's hooded cape and wings. And like a Barbie doll for middle-agers, she comes with a complete story line. The attached booklet described some of her mischievous "feats" this way:

> With a touch of her magic wand, she zaps your estrogen, taking it with her in the hope of someday using it to recapture her own long-lost youth. Now, you may ask, "How can I tell if I've been zapped by the Estrogen Fairy?" Well, if you've ever experienced one of these symptoms, you can bet she's the culprit:

- You find yourself in the garage and don't know whether you're on your way out or you've already been there and had a good time.

- You burst into tears when the traffic light turns red.

- You go to bed feeling peaceful yet awaken thinking the world (and everyone in it) is falling apart and you're positive it's your fault.

**The Estrogen Fairy**

- The only men who smile at you are plastic surgeons.[12]

Here are some other signs that you're living somewhere between estrogen and death:

- When you do the "Hokey Pokey," you put your left hip out . . . and it stays there.
- You run out of breath walking *down* a flight of stairs.
- Classmates at your reunion think you're one of their former teachers.

As we grow older, everything slows down—including our mental processes. Bill and I have noticed this phenomenon as we enjoy one of our favorite TV game shows—*Jeopardy!* Recently I noticed I was a bit late with the answers . . . sometimes by two or three days! Then one night I was *amazed* that I knew almost all the answers. Later I realized it was a rerun from the week before!

We're all aware of the years passing by. But just when do we become *old*? How do we know when we've reached that stage? One jokester said you know you're getting old when you yearn for those blessed old hymns of days gone by, especially:

- "Go Tell It on the Mountain—and Speak Up!"

- "Nobody Knows the Trouble I Have Seeing"

- "Guide Me, O Thou Great Jehovah (I've Forgotten Where I Parked)"

It's not as if we're the only ones trying to figure out when old age hits. Awhile back when Bill had to have some medical tests, the doctor's nurse called to explain the procedure and what he needed to do before and after the tests. Knowing Bill is living somewhere between geriatric junction and heaven's pearly gates, the *real* reason for the nurse's call to me was apparently to determine whether I was capable of following her instructions and taking care of his needs. We made small talk for a minute or two before she finally drew in a breath and said, "Well, you sound pretty *spry!*"

Humorist Dave Barry says old age begins the first time you put on a pair of reading glasses. He compares this transformation to the same one Clark Kent went through, only in reverse: "He takes off his glasses and becomes Superman; you put on your reading glasses and become . . . Old Person." But this transformation doesn't happen overnight, of course. For Barry, it began in restaurants when he was forty-eight:

> At first I thought that this had nothing to do with me— that, for some reason, possibly to save ink, the restaurants had started printing their menus in letters the height of bacteria; all I could see was little blurs. But for some reason, everybody else seemed to be able to read the menus. Not wishing to draw attention to myself, I started ordering my food by simply pointing to a likely looking blur.

*Me (pointing to a blur):* I'll have this.

*Waiter:* You'll have "We Do Not Accept Personal Checks"?

*Me:* Make that medium rare.

Pretty soon I started noticing that everything I tried to read—newspapers, books, nasal-spray instructions, the U.S. Constitution—had been changed to the bacteria-letter format. I also discovered that, contrary to common sense, I could read these letters if I got farther away from them. So for a while I dealt with the situation by ordering off the menus of people sitting at other tables.

"I'd like to order some dessert," I'd tell the waiter. "Please bring a menu to the people at that table over there and ask them to hold it up so I can see it."[13]

"I've reached the age where
I need three pairs of glasses:
One for driving, one for reading—
and one to find the other two!"

## Snappy Birthday Greetings

Many of us especially feel ourselves whizzing through the aging turnstiles when we celebrate (or endure) birthdays ending with zeros. Actually, these events might not seem as monumental to us except for the wisecracks of our so-called friends, the ones who delight in sending us those sarcastic greeting cards that start ribbing us about getting old when we first turn thirty. By the time we're forty, they're downright wicked. Author Max Lucado said he received these happy birthday wishes when he reached the big four-oh:

- You know you're getting older when you try to straighten out the wrinkles in your socks only to find you aren't wearing any.

- At twenty we don't care what the world thinks of us; at thirty we start to worry about what the world thinks of us; at forty we realize the world isn't thinking of us at all.

- I've gotten to the age where I need my false teeth and hearing aid before I can ask where I left my glasses.

- Forty is when you stop patting yourself on the back and start patting yourself under the chin.[14]

The smart-aleck cards continue for decades. And then an interesting thing happens. It would seem like a relief, except that we *know* what it *really* means when the greeting-card humor dries up. The kidding stops, and the greeting cards take on a kinder, gentler tone (with bigger, bolder letters). That's the indication that we've reached the point when it's not safe to make wisecracks because the things that were once so funny on the earlier greeting cards are now *true!*

One greeting-card company spokesman said age forty used to be the company's cutoff for printing cards with humorous slams about getting old. Now, he said, fifty-year-olds "are able to take kidding. . . . We tend to tone it down a little at fifty, but not much. At sixty, it's definitely toned down. And that's where [the company's humor division] stops doing milestone cards." Another card company follows the same philosophy. After fifty, a card company editor said, "We enter Compliment City." That's when the wisecracks turn into compliments: "You're looking marvelous" or "What a great year you've had!"[15]

*Compliment City?* How awful!

It's strange, isn't it, the way we look at aging? Someone sent me a little essay that notes when we're kids, we *want* to get old. In fact, kids younger than ten give their age in fractions: "I'm four and a half." We're even more forward-focused as teenagers, automatically jumping to the next number: "I'm almost sixteen." Then comes twenty-one, and we've peaked. After that, the verbs start taking on a rather negative tone as we mark each milestone:

We *turn* thirty (makes you sound like milk that turned bad). The next thing we know, we're *pushing* forty. Then we *reach* fifty, *hit* sixty, *make it to* seventy, and *live until* our eighties. After that, a strange thing happens. We start going backward, telling listeners, "I was ninety-two in April."

These stages keep coming so quickly, you may not even realize they're taking you into old age. Here's the way one writer told Ann Landers how to know you're getting old:

- The magic begins. You put your keys on the dresser, and they mysteriously wind up on top of the fridge. You lay the remote on the TV and find it later under the sofa. You slip your wallet into your purse, and the next morning it is on the front seat of your car.

- You do a lot of arithmetic. "Let's see, he died, and he was—and I am four years younger, so that means she is—and I'm—no way! Not possible." . . .

- You develop TMI (Too Much Information), a sure sign of old age. I remind myself that every happening need not be reported in endless detail.

- You laugh at yourself more. Be grateful that you can. Some people can't. If you are unable to find the humor in yourself, chances are you won't find it anywhere else. The alternative is anger and despair.[16]

That kind of attitude was expressed in the happy demeanor of an old lady in the nursing home where my sister Janet goes every week to play the piano for the residents. One week the ninety-three-year-old woman told Janet, "I get up every morning and look in the mirror, and I know who I am. And I see the calendar and know what day it is. And then I say, 'Well, praise the Lord!'"

In contrast, there was Bill Cosby's grandfather. When someone asked him, on his ninety-eighth birthday, "How does it feel to be ninety-eight?" the old man replied gruffly, "It wasn't worth the wait!"

## Looking Back in Awe

Imagine what it's like for these witty elders to think back on the changes they've witnessed. When we were in Nebraska last year, an Omaha woman told me how her grandmother had marveled that she lived long enough to see covered wagons . . . and the space shuttle. Soon after that, I read a newspaper story announcing the recent death, at age ninety, of the first patient whose life was saved by penicillin back in 1942. And not long after that I saw an article that named an American company that has committed $500 million to "build a cruise ship to ferry people from Earth orbit to the moon and back" and another company that "confirmed that it is looking into the feasibility of a space hotel."[17]

Such stories reminded me of all the things we gained during the last century. But we lost some things too. When *USA Today* asked its readers last year what they would miss in this new millennium, one of the surprising things they mentioned was *stars!* Apparently many of the respondents had grown up in a more rural era, and they remembered standing in the yards of their remote farmhouses at night and seeing the beautiful canopy of the universe twinkling overhead. Now, in many places, the stars are dimmed, the writer noted, "their spectacular nightly show hidden behind the glare of city lights."[18]

This little "test" someone sent to me reminds us of some of the other things that disappeared with the turn of the century—or earlier. See which ones you remember:

1. Blackjack chewing gum
2. Little Coke-shaped bottles made of wax with colored sugar water inside
3. Soda pop machines that dispensed glass bottles
4. Home milk delivery in glass bottles with cardboard caps
5. Telephone party lines
6. Newsreels before movies
7. P.F. Flyers

8. Butch Wax
9. Telephone numbers with a word prefix (Olive 2-6933 or Tuxedo 4-9351)
10. Peashooters
11. Howdy Doody
12. 45 RPM and 78 RPM Records
13. Metal ice trays with levers
14. Mimeograph machines
15. Blue flashbulbs
16. Beanie and Cecil
17. Roller-skate keys
18. Cork popguns
19. Studebakers
20. Wringer washtubs

Count how many of these items you remember to know how old you really are:

**0:** You're still young.
**1–10:** You're getting older
**11–15:** Don't tell your age.
**More than 15:** You're older than dirt!

There probably was a time, perhaps back at the *last* turn of the century, when those wringer washtubs were considered modern miracles. One woman told me her pioneer grandmother used to regale her with stories of taking the family's clothes and bedding to the creek several times a year to do the laundry. She dipped creek water into iron kettles, built a fire, boiled the clothes, scrubbed them with homemade lye soap, and then had to wring out everything—including the heavy quilts—by hand. To those hardworking women, wringer washtubs were probably a modern miracle!

© 1999. Reprinted courtesy of Bunny Hoest and *Parade* magazine.

"Some would say I'm retired, but I like to think of
myself as a stay-at-home grandfather."

In the same way, we still have many advances to be thankful for, even as we lament beloved things we've had to give up. A recent newspaper clipping reminded me of this kind of blessing. It described a seventy-year-old woman—a woman born long before penicillin, computers, and many other modern medical advances—who had lost almost all of her hearing nearly twenty years earlier. Since then she had had a tiny bit of hearing in one ear but had been functionally deaf. She used a writing board to communicate with her family.

Then she learned of a new type of surgical technology that would insert a tiny, computerized device in her head that *might* restore her hearing. Or it might not. In fact, there was an almost certain risk that the operation would destroy the tiny bit of hearing she still had, so if the implanted device didn't work she would be totally deaf. But being a courageous woman, she decided to take that risk. She wasn't just courageous, though. She was a Christian. And on the morning of her surgery, the woman's daughter opened her book of daily readings and was amazed to find, in that day's selection, this verse from Isaiah 48:6: "From this time forward, I will make you hear new things, hidden things that you have not known."

It took several weeks after the surgery for the incision to heal and the device to be turned on so it could begin working. And on that morning when the doctor finally attempted to activate the implant, the woman and her family rejoiced when, for the first time in two decades, she heard her loved ones' voices again.[19]

Don't you love stories like that? Courageous people of all ages are inspiring to the rest of us. But when they're seventy years old, they're more than courageous. They're heroes.

Of course, being one who loves to laugh, I can't help but throw in here the joke about the old man who had had a serious hearing loss for many years. He finally went to the doctor and was fitted for a set of hearing aids that restored his hearing completely. When the old man went back to the doctor a month later for a checkup, the doctor said, "Your hearing is perfect. Your family must be really pleased that you can hear again."

"Oh, I haven't told them yet," the old man replied. "I just sit around and listen. I've changed my will three times!"

That old guy had discovered a wonderful insight that many of us would be wise to share. Some of us, especially as we get older, seem to have no interest in *listening*. We only want others to listen to us. But if we would just stop yapping for a minute and really *hear* what our friends and loved ones are telling us, we might learn something—or maybe even something that would prompt us to change our wills!

### Saturated Brain Storage

Hearing about the implant that miraculously restored the deaf woman's hearing, I can't help but wish scientists would develop some kind of brain implant we could get to ward off memory loss as we age. One comedian said that older people "lose their memory because their brains are full, often with useless data such as the name of their third grade teacher and the lyrics to 'Volare.'" Well, I can't sing "Volare," but I can name my former teachers—and I have no idea where I just left my glasses . . . or my checkbook . . . or my car keys. So maybe the comedian is right when he suggests that what we need is a form of add-on storage space for our brains, along the lines of those storage sheds people erect in their backyards. Or, he said, we might somehow "download" surplus information to our stomachs, "where there is plenty of room."[20]

Think about it. If only we had more room to store the things we want to remember, we'd actually get our money's worth from those memory-enhancing courses that are so popular now. One elderly couple, getting on in years and losing their memories, decided to take such a course. The husband was thrilled with the results; in fact, he felt the course changed his life. He and his wife met their friend Bill on the street, and the husband said to him, "Bill, you just have to take this incredible memory course my wife and I just finished. It's fantastic! You won't believe the improvement."

Bill said, "Wow! That's great. What's the name of the course?"

The husband turned to his wife and asked, "What's the name of that flower? You know, the one with the long stem and the thorns?"

"You mean a rose?" his wife replied.

"Yeah, that's it! (pause . . .) Rose, what was the name of that memory course?"

## Aging Gracefully
One of the things I hope I can remember is the advice that Dear Abby columnist Abigail Van Buren gave when she celebrated her eightieth birthday. Asked to name her biggest accomplishment, she answered succinctly, "Surviving." Then she shared her advice for aging gracefully:

Fear less; hope more. Eat less; chew more. Talk less; say more. Hate less; love more. And never underestimate the power of forgiveness.

## Squirts & Squints

Bumper sticker:
JESUS IS COMING! LOOK BUSY!

A reporter was visiting an elderly couple who had just celebrated their sixty-fifth wedding anniversary. He was touched by the way the husband continually spoke to his wife in terms of endearment, always calling her "Sweetheart," "Honey," or "Dear."

"It's so sweet, the way you address your wife in those endearing ways," the reporter said to the husband.

"Well, to tell you the truth," the old man answered, "I forgot her name about ten years ago."

I can see clearly now. My brain is gone.

### Top Ten Reasons Why Heaven's Looking Good

10. You can begin the Lord's Prayer, "Our Father, who art here . . ."
9. You can find out the answer to the question "Why?"
8. Wings.
7. Soul music for eternity.
6. Real golden arches.
5. Great view.
4. "No pain, no gain" becomes "no pain, no pain."
3. When you say, "Oh, God . . ." you'll hear, "Yes?"
2. Harp lessons.

And the number one reason why heaven's looking good:
1. It's totally fat free.

—FRED W. SANFORD

It is easier to get older than wiser.

Some people grow up and spread cheer . . .
Others just grow up and spread.

**SHOE**

© Tribune Media Services, Inc. All Rights Reserved. Reprinted with permission.

The glory of each morning
is that it offers us a chance to begin again.

As an aircraft landed at the airport, a flight attendant made this announcement:

> "Ladies and gentlemen, we have a very special person on board this evening. He is ninety-six years old today, and this is his very first flight. As you deplane this evening, please stop by the cockpit and wish our captain Happy Birthday!"

It's not the pace of life that concerns me,
it's the sudden stop at the end.

Three friends were talking about death. One of them asked, "When you are in your casket and friends and family are mourning over you, what would you most like to hear them say about you? I've been thinking about it, and I hope they'll say that I was one of the great doctors of my time—and a great family man."

The second man said, "I would like to hear them say that I was a loving husband and father, and a devoted schoolteacher who made a difference in shaping the adults of tomorrow."

The third man thought seriously for a moment and then said, "I would like to hear them say . . . 'LOOK, HE'S MOVING! HE'S STILL ALIVE!'"

Two bikers were riding down a country road on a Harley. The driver's leather jacket wouldn't stay closed because the zipper had broken, so he pulled over. "Just put your jacket on backward," his buddy suggested.

Then they zoomed off down the road, until they hit a curve at high speed and crashed. A farmer found them and called the police.

"Is either of them showing any sign of life?" asked the officer.

"Well, the first one was," replied the farmer, "until I turned his head around the right way."[21]

Have you heard about the new Barbie dolls?

*Bifocals Barbie:* Comes with her own set of bifocal fashion frames in six wild colors (half-frames too!), neck chain, and large-print editions of *Vogue* and *Martha Stewart Living.*

*Hot Flash Barbie:* Press Barbie's bellybutton, and watch her face turn beet red while tiny drops of perspiration appear on her forehead. Comes with handheld fan and tiny tissues.

*Facial Hair Barbie:* As Barbie's hormone levels shift, see her whiskers grow. Available with teensy tweezers and magnifying mirror.

*Bunion Barbie:* Years of disco dancing in stiletto heels have taken their toll on Barbie's dainty, arched feet. Soothe her sores with the pumice stone and plasters, then slip on soft terry slippers.

*No-More-Wrinkles Barbie:* Erase those pesky crow's-feet and lip lines with a tube of Skin Sparkle-Spackle from Barbie's own line of exclusive age-blasting cosmetics.

*Post-Menopausal Barbie:* She wets her pants when she sneezes, forgets where she put things, and cries a lot. Comes with micro-Depends and Kleenex.

A little boy took his pet iguana to school to show the other kids. If you've ever seen an iguana, you know it has a large flap of skin, called the dewlap, that hangs down from the neck. The kids asked what it was, and when the boy explained, a little girl said, "Oh! My grandma has one of those."

When did my wild oats
turn into shredded wheat?

Post Mark Twain's wisdom on your mirror and practice adding facial creases each day: "Wrinkles merely indicate where the smiles have been."

Praise the LORD, O my soul, and forget not all his benefits.

—PSALM 103:2

# Sliding Down a Rainbow, into a Pool of Joy!

## *"That's What It's All About, Isn't It, Barb?"*

**W**hen Sam Butcher, the creator of Precious Moments, gave me permission to use some of his adorable artwork in my book *He's Gonna Toot and I'm Gonna Scoot!* I was overjoyed. He even invited us to come to the fabulous Precious Moments Chapel outside Carthage, Missouri, to get better acquainted with his work—and with him. We had such a marvelous time there seeing the chapel, the breathtaking fountain event, and even his own private art gallery and visiting with Sam and his super-efficient assistant Larrene Hagaman, that I wanted to reciprocate. "You've gotta come to a Women of Faith conference," I begged, "so I can introduce you to a few thousand of *my* friends."

Larrene told "the rest of the story" about Sam's appearance at the Kansas City conference in May 1999 in an article she wrote for *Chapel Bells* magazine, and she's agreed to let me adapt it here for you to enjoy:

The mere thought of being present with over eighteen thousand women was enough to give Mr. Butcher a chill, but when Barbara implied he might want to say something, he really got the "willies"! At first he agreed that if my husband, Darrell, could go along, he would go and be willing to be introduced, stand, and wave. Then he got braver and said he would "say a little something."

Kemper Arena in Kansas City is a huge, round building, and as we met Barbara, her husband, Bill, and the others, Mr. B said, "I really need more time to think about what I'm going to say."

Loosely translated, I have come to know that means he needs to pace—and I need to be sociable. I gathered with several others in the green room and discovered that Barbara was nearly as nervous as he was! This is not the norm for Barbara, who will speak in over thirty cities this year with audiences ranging from eight to twenty thousand people. But introducing Mr. Butcher made her more nervous than if she were "introducing Billy Graham or the Pope," she said as we left the room and began to walk back and forth in the hallway, straining to see which direction Mr. B had gone. It was a long, long hallway that circled the entire building.

I tried to soothe Barbara, and we moved back into the green room to join the others. "The neat thing about these conferences," one of the ladies said, "is that all the men's bathrooms are turned into women's!"

My eyes widened as that thought penetrated my brain and I realized Mr. B *didn't know* that potentially catastrophic little fact! I ran out the door, grabbed Darrell and said, "You go that way, and I'll go this way! Find Mr. Butcher, and don't either of you go to the bathroom!"

Darrell thought I'd lost my marbles, but he dutifully headed out, found the boss, and much to my relief, both of them returned unscathed.

It wasn't long until we were swooped into the midst of eighteen thousand rousing, clapping, joyous women who were swinging with the gospel group that was leading into Barbara's segment of this whopper of a gathering. Mr. B was mentally still gathering his thoughts right up until he was introduced. And, as usual, he gathered them in a way that was just right. He endeared himself to everyone when he pointed to the words he had written on his hand and shyly said, "My notes!"

Part of what he shared was a real surprise for Barbara. He announced that this year's charity doll would have a specific name for the first time, and that the proceeds would go to assist her Spatula Ministries.*

The "Barbara Charity Doll" is really a beauty. It has a straw hat with a red geranium on it, and it is holding a spatula. Barbara's best-selling book, *Stick a Geranium in Your Hat and Be Happy*, led to her being well known as the "Geranium Lady." Her ministry is to assist parents who learn something about their children that they find so shocking, they need someone to scrape them off the ceiling with a spatula of love. Barbara often receives calls and letters from parents of gays, lesbians, young people who have joined occult groups, etc. She assists in so many ways to help those who have AIDS and their families as well. In fact, each December she personally telephones hundreds who have lost a child and are struggling to survive, to tell them that she remembers and is thinking of them. That phone bill alone is well over five thousand dollars!

The vice president of Word Publishing, Joey Paul, presented Mr. Butcher a plaque showing the cover of *Toot and Scoot* and a perfectly charming drawing of the Geranium Lady bending over to kiss Timmy the Angel. It will be hung in the gallery near the chapel for everyone to enjoy.

After the presentation, we slipped away to a lovely, historic restaurant several miles from the arena. Sue Ann Jones, Barbara's editor, explained that at the arena the

---

* For details about ordering the Precious Moments "Barbara Johnson Charity Doll (PMC 1145)" call 1-800-445-2220 or go to www.preciousmoments.com.

night before a sweet Precious Moments collector, Sarah Rawley, had bought a copy of *Toot and Scoot* at Barbara's book table and was so excited to learn that Mr. Butcher would be present the next day. When she asked if he was going to be signing, Sue Ann told her no, but being the kind person that she is, she offered to take the girl's book and see if Mr. B would sign it during the luncheon.

As we walked into the restaurant and made our way to a private dining room in another area, Sue Ann expressed complete surprise to find Sarah sitting in this restaurant, miles from the arena, with her friends and family. (She learned later that Sarah's mother had made *their* reservations long before the event and had no idea we would be there either!)

As we settled into our private dining room, Mr. B took off his suit coat and rolled up his shirt sleeves, grateful for a moment of "down time" after the excitement of the jam-packed arena. After Sue Ann told me about the situation with the girl out in the main dining room, I assured her that Mr. Butcher would no doubt want to sign the book for her—and deliver it personally! Such was the case! As soon as he heard about Sarah, he quickly signed a brief dedication, re-buttoned his shirt cuffs, reached for his coat, and beckoned for Sue Ann to come and point Sarah out to him. Knowing Sarah would want a photographic remembrance of the moment, he said, "Larrene, don't forget the camera!" as he headed out the door.

So we all trooped back out toward the main dining room, intending to peek around the door while Sue Ann pointed out Sarah to Sam. But as soon as their heads poked around the edge, Sarah spotted them and popped to her feet. She'd been watching that door!

With a broad smile, Mr. B presented the signed book to Sarah, then we snapped the photo shown here—and made Sarah's day!

Later, Barbara told Mr. B how special she thought it

*Sam Butcher's thoughtful kindness touched Sarah Rawley's heart—and mine.*

was of him to make that extra effort. His response was so typical of him. "That's what it's all about, isn't it, Barbara?" he said.

As she nodded, I thought how blessed I am to call each of them my friend.[1]

My friendship with Sam Butcher and his incredible assistant, Larrene, has been a "bath of blessings" for me. To be honest, after twenty years of working with hurting families and heartbroken parents, I thought I knew a lot about serving others through ministry. But every time I'm with Sam, I'm inspired and educated. In Kansas City when he said, "That's what it's all about, isn't it, Barb?" I saw the incredible power of his servant's heart. Sam's right. As Christians, serving others is exactly what it's all about for all of us!

By his kind thoughtfulness, Sam demonstrates the truth of the following "gift list" put together by an unknown writer:

### Priceless Gifts to Give for Free

*The gift of listening:* No interrupting, no daydreaming, no planning your responses. Just listen.

*The gift of affection:* Be generous with appropriate hugs, kisses, pats on the back, and handholds. Let these small actions demonstrate the love you have for family and friends.

*The gift of laughter:* Share articles, funny stories, and cartoons to tell someone, "I love to laugh with you."

*The gift of a written note:* A brief, handwritten note may be remembered for a lifetime and may even change a life.

*The gift of a compliment:* A simple and sincere "You look great in red," "You did a super job," or "That was a wonderful meal" can make someone's day.

*The gift of a favor:* Every day, go out of your way to do something kind for someone.

*The gift of solitude:* There are times when we want nothing more than to be left alone. Be sensitive to those times and give the gift of solitude to others.

*The gift of a cheerful disposition:* The easiest way to feel good is to extend a kind word to someone, even if it's just saying hello or thank you.

*The gift of a prayer:* Let your friends and loved ones know you pray for them—and then do it!

## Reaching Out . . .

We like to say that Spatula Ministries uses a spatula of love to scrape parents down when something about their children has caused them to land on the ceiling. Sometimes these ceiling-flattened parents are trying to cope with adult children who are struggling with AIDS, addictions, prostitution, cults, and all sorts of other problems that cause many folks, even Christians, to reject them and heap scorn upon them—and sometimes upon their parents too. That's why I was so touched last year when a friend added this postscript to her letter:

Barbara, keep doing what you do. There are churches and Christian programs around the world that minister to the ninety-and-nine. But you are reaching out to that one lost sheep.

My friend's encouragement reminded me that it might be *my* arms reaching out to that "one lost sheep," but it's God's love flowing through me that accomplishes the healing. As someone said,

Broken skin heals in days . . . broken bones in weeks or months . . . broken hearts and spirits sometimes in years . . . broken souls heal only by God's grace.

Sam Butcher shares my concern for the outcast. Larrene loaned me a tape of a message Sam gave recently about the story of the leper in the first chapter of the Gospel of Mark. Sam noted that the leper lived each day with three condemnations. He was condemned by his own deadly afflictions, by his friends and family, and by society and the law. In Jesus' day, lepers were totally shunned; some people feared that they might be contaminated if they even looked at a leper.

Keep this situation in mind, Sam said, as you picture Jesus surrounded by a crowd of people, all wanting something from Him. Suddenly the crowd parted as the believers pushed and shoved to keep from touching the one lone leper who was courageously making his way toward Jesus. The others struggled to get away from the leper, but Jesus remained. And then He did something that astonished those watching. The Bible says Jesus, "filled with compassion, . . . reached out his hand and touched the man."[2]

A simple touch . . . but what a difference it made.

Jesus' example shows that serving others with a humble heart doesn't mean we have to do great, extravagant things to

I know the Lord is my shepherd...

Sometimes I just really
look forward to lying down in
those green pastures by
that quiet stream, don't you?!

Art and copy by Matt Anderson. Used by permission. © DaySpring® Cards, Siloam Springs, Arkansas.

do what Jesus would do. Sometimes we can simply touch the untouchable . . . and share God's loving, life-changing grace.

We do God's work because God promises to work in us and through us. What a comfort to consider this list someone compiled of the promises He has made to us:

## God's Promises

I will never leave you nor forsake you. (Josh. 1:5)

I will sustain you and rescue you. (Isa. 46:4)

I will strengthen you and help you; I will uphold you with my righteous right hand. (Isa. 41:10)

I am with you and will watch over you wherever you go. (Gen. 28:15)

I am your hiding place. I will protect you from trouble and surround you with songs of deliverance. I will instruct you and teach you in the way you should go; I will counsel you and watch over you. (Ps. 32:7–8)

Call to me and I will answer you and tell you great and unsearchable things you do not know. (Jer. 33:3)

I am with you, I am mighty to save. I will take great delight in you. I will quiet you with my love. I will rejoice over you with singing. (Zeph. 3:17)

**The Smallest Gesture**
After our son Steven was killed in Vietnam, he was buried with military honors in a local cemetery. My memory of that day is a blur of painful yet encouraging scenes. But the most memorable moment for me lasted no more than a second; it was a tiny gesture of respect that has comforted me for nearly thirty years. At the end of the military salute at the cemetery, the honor guard precisely folded the flag covering Steven's casket. Next it was passed to the leader of the honor guard, who turned sharply and then slowly walked the few steps to where our family was seated. It was the split-second gesture the soldier made before giving us the flag that has stayed with me all these years. He touched the folded flag to his heart, held it there for only a second, and then extended it to Bill.

You may never know who or how others will be affected by the simplest gesture of kindness or the briefest message of hope. After including in my conference message the story of how some of the Women of Faith gals had reached out to help a desperate prostitute with full-blown AIDS who had stumbled into the arena where the event was being held, someone left this note at my book table.

> Dear Barbara,
> Thank you. I am a police officer and a mother of four. My 21-year-old daughter is a crack-addicted prostitute. Thank you for the hope.

You see, when I told that story to the audience of ten thousand women, I thought I was delivering a motivational message—an encouragement to those women to put the idea of

"What Would Jesus Do?" into action. But to one woman I was sharing a message of hope—the hope that somewhere out there, a kind, Christian soul might also show kindness to *her* daughter, wherever she was, and lead her to Christ.

A similar thing happened when the Women of Faith tour was in a southern city a couple of years ago. My hostess there was a wonderfully efficient professional woman who not only made the conference go smoothly for us but also gave us a delightful tour of the city and nearby plantations and shared with us the stories of her own amazing ancestors. She knew very little about my books or my ministry that reaches out to the families of homosexuals. In fact, she knew very little about "that lifestyle" at all—except, she said, she'd had a cousin, an entertainer, who'd lived a rather unusual existence.

She was driving my helpers and me from the hotel to the arena as she told us the story. Her entertainer cousin, she said, had undergone one of the first sex-change operations several years earlier. Then he had become a Christian and had had the operation reversed, all in the glare of publicity that had embarrassed his whole family. "We all knew about it," the hostess said, "but no one talked about him anymore. It was as though he didn't really exist. But he was always so dear to me. We had been friends as children, and I just loved him right up until his death a few years ago," she said sadly.

My antenna had gone up as soon as she started laying out the details of the entertainer's story. "What was his name?" I asked.

"Perry Desmond," she answered simply.

"Perry Desmond!? Perry *Desmond?* Oh, of course I knew Perry Desmond!" I exclaimed. "I loved him! He and I did some programs together. In fact, we shared a room together once. We got to the hotel somewhere, and there weren't enough rooms, and no one would share with him—you know he *was* a little strange—and I said, 'Well, I'll room with him—or her—or whatever he was at that moment.' He was so much fun, and he had so much talent. And when he died, we had a little service for him out in California, just his close friends and the people he had worked with. I think I've still got the videotape we made of all the funny things and tributes his friends made for him."

Hearing my excited babbling, the hostess burst into tears! I couldn't imagine what I'd said that was so bad. But finally she managed to say, "Oh, Barb! I loved Perry, and it hurt me to see how he was treated by everyone, including his family. You can't imagine what it means to me to know that he had friends like you . . . that there were people out there who were kind to him."

**That's Life**

"Have a nice eternity."

Having a son who's a homosexual, I know how hurtful it is to imagine him being scorned or ridiculed. Now whenever I see or meet a person who's obviously struggling with homosexuality or "gender identity," as they say, I no longer think, *What a strange person that is!* Instead I quickly remember, *That person is some poor mother's child.* And that attitude, I've found, makes quite a difference in my actions. It's an idea that is expressed so beautifully in this essay by an unknown writer:

You see her, don't You, Lord Jesus? She's standing there, alone, on the edge of the playground, a forlorn little waif who's not quite right. Her clothes aren't right, her hair isn't right, and her speech . . . well, it isn't right, either.

You know her, Lord. A bypassed, misfit little duckling, standing all alone because the other ducklings say she's not quite right.

What can I do, Lord? I can't force the other kids to include her in their merry game. That would only make matters worse, turning a harsh spotlight on her misery.

Seeing her standing there, I swallow hard, bite my lip, and look away. Oh, Lord Jesus, why? Why are there outcasts on the edge of the playground, on the edge of the neighborhood, the edge of the church? If I were in charge, there'd be none of that. No one would be lonely just because her clothes weren't right, her hair was funny, and her speech came with a lisp. If it were *my* world, all the ducklings would be, well, *acceptable* . . .

But I know Your ways are not my ways, Lord. I want acceptable ducklings, while You want glorious swans. You want Your ducklings to know the infinite value of being weak, humble, and not quite "right." You want us to understand that the pain of being different just might be Your way of preparing us for greatness.

Lord, please help me to see that lonely little girl through Your eyes. Show me the promise in her humility, the talents hidden within her so that I can help her see them too. Help me to give her . . . herself.

Thank You for reminding me that no one loves the outcast more than You do, Lord Jesus. No one is more sensitive to the abandoned and the lonely than You, who stretched out Your arms on the cross to gather the outcasts, the misfits, the lepers, the maimed, and the funny-looking.

Oh, Jesus! Open Your arms again and gather in that forlorn little girl . . . and me.

## Blessed to be a Blessing

As someone said, the opportunity to do good is so fleeting. It's not enough to see the little, lonely girl and have our hearts broken. We have to do more than grieve for her and pray for her. We have to *touch* her in some way, just as Jesus reached out and touched the leper.

At the National Prayer Breakfast last year, one of the speakers said, "Each one of us has a unique assignment in this world given to us by a sovereign God—to love and to serve those within our own sphere of influence. We've been blessed to be a blessing; we've received that we might give."

More times than I can recount, I know I have "received that I might give"; I've been blessed to be a blessing. Here's one way someone's gesture of kindness to me has descended through the years to be a blessing to others like a pebble dropped in a pond.

The story began in 1973 when our son Tim and another friend were in their early twenties and traveled to Alaska for one of those classic adventures of youth. They planned to just stay a short while, see the sights, and come home. But at a gas station in Anchorage, they happened to meet a friendly resident who noticed their California license plate and commented on how far they had driven. Despite my best efforts during Tim's childhood to train him not to go home with strangers, he and his friend accepted the man's invitation to go to his house for dinner. He was a youth minister, he told them, and some other young people were coming over that night for a Bible study get-together.

The boys must have enjoyed the evening. They not only stayed for dinner—they stayed two months! The thoughtful youth minister, Ted McReynolds, and his wife, Joanne, opened their home to these young adventurers so far from home. While they were staying with Ted and Joanne, Tim's life changed. He'd been raised as a Christian, but there in Alaska, with Ted and Joanne leading the way, his spiritual life ignited, and he was on fire for Jesus. While he was up there he was baptized. And he rededicated his life to the Lord.

(I was a little hurt by that. I thought, *Our church has good water down here.*) I was eager to have him come home and tell us all about his experiences.

After he'd left Alaska and was driving back to California, he called about midday from White Horse in the Yukon Territory of Canada and told me, "Mom, I have a spring in my step and a sparkle in my eye. I'll be home in five days and tell you all about it!"

We were so eager to see him and hear how God had worked in his life. But it wasn't to be. A few hours later, while we were eating dinner, we got a call from the Royal Canadian Mounted Police telling us that Tim and his friend had been killed in a crash with a drunk driver.

During the awful time after the accident, Ted and Joanne McReynolds called from Alaska. They wanted to come to California and tell us what had happened to Tim—in other words, they wanted to tell the story of Tim's experiences in Alaska that Tim himself had been so eager to tell us. After meeting them, we asked Ted to help conduct the boys' service. It was a tremendous outpouring of hope as he told the story of how Tim had dedicated his future to living for Jesus.

Inspired by Ted and Joanne's example, I resolved right then and there to reach out to other parents in pain and offer the kind of encouragement and hope they had given us. Wherever and whenever I could, I wanted to help other parents whose hearts had been broken by the loss of a child. Bill and I had already taken a few steps in that direction five years earlier when Steven died in Vietnam, but now we worked with renewed purpose. Later, when a third son, Larry, disappeared into the homosexual lifestyle, our work expanded to include *those* parents too.

Looking back now, I recognize that gift of encouragement from Ted and Joanne as the pebble tossed into a pool. Their kindness splashed over me in a ripple of love. And I have been blessed, in the twenty-six years since then, with the honor of splashing those ripples on to others. The result has been more than a dozen books—now totaling more than five million copies in print—plus several years of nationwide speaking appearances and thousands of contacts with parents who have lost their children to death or alienation due to homosexuality or other situations. In addition, I've been a guest on dozens of TV and radio shows across the land, spreading the encouraging message of hope that was handed down to me by the McReynoldses all those years ago.

One of those radio shows came back to me as a boomerang blessing last year when the Women of Faith tour was in Denver. As a result, someone else dropped in another pebble of hope to keep the blessing going. And along the way, I had a little adventure of my own!

This part of the story actually began about fifteen years ago—five years after the McReynoldses had inspired me to pass along their blessing of hope. A young doctor was driving from Houston to San Francisco. His younger brother had committed suicide, and he was on his way up there to plan the service and pull everybody together. He turned on the radio in his car on his way up there, and it happened to be playing a *Focus on the Family* program. It was actually a tape that had been made a few months earlier when I'd been a guest on the show. On the tape Dr. James Dobson was asking me, "Barb, how do you deal with the families of those who have committed suicide?"

I answered that I remind parents that when someone commits suicide he "goes out to meet a just and a loving God." And then I said some other things about counseling those families who have gone through that situation.

At the end of the program, Dr. Dobson, bless his heart, gave out my home phone number! This young doctor, driving from Texas to California, heard my number, got off the freeway, stopped at a pay phone, and called me. He said, "My brother committed suicide, and I'm on my way to organize his funeral. I've never done this before. I don't know what to say, but you were a ministering angel to me today, Barbara. Everything you said I can put together for his memorial service. I just had to call and tell you how you ministered to me today—without even knowing it."

Sometime later I visited the doctor in Houston and spoke at his church, and then he came to our home and visited us. We became friends. He would call me every few weeks and say, "I need a couple of boxes of your books. I have a lot of patients who have problems!"

So, over the next fifteen years, we kept him supplied with books for his patients. Then, just a few years ago, he moved to the Denver area.

When the Women of Faith tour was in Denver last fall, our MC, Mary Graham, became incapacitated with severe leg cramps. When I heard about it, I rushed to Mary's room, took one look at her, and even though it was eleven o'clock at night, I called my doctor friend, Doug.

Right away he said, "Barbara, what can I do for you? You've been a ministering angel to me for all these years. Can I be your ministering angel *now?*"

"Oh, yes!" I answered. "I need help, because this woman, Mary, is not only my dear friend, she's in charge of this whole conference! And she can hardly walk. She's having terrible trouble, and oh, I hope you can help her. But I've already called two or three drugstores, and there's nothing open around here this late at night. I can't even get aspirin!"

He said, "You just hang on. I'll call her and make sure I understand what her problem is. Then I'll call a Walgreen's that's open all night. It's not in the safest area, Barb, but if you can get over there, they'll have the prescriptions waiting for you."

I said, "Doug, I've already gone to bed. I've got no car or anything. How am I gonna get over there?"

He said, "Oh, you'll figure that out, Barb. I know you. Now, I'll call in the prescriptions, but I also want you to get her some ripe bananas. She needs to eat something with this medication, and bananas would be best."

Ripe bananas? At eleven o'clock at night when I can't even find a drugstore, I had to find ripe bananas too? But I called a cab and rushed downstairs. In the lobby I met Liz, a Campus Crusade worker who helps with the conferences. She was just coming in from the airport. She took one look at me—I was wearing Bill's shirt over my slacks, had on no makeup, and hadn't fixed my hair since getting out of bed—and said, "Barb! What's wrong?"

I told her the whole story, and she said, "I'll take you to Walgreen's."

"They say it's in a dangerous part of town," I warned.

Liz answered, "That's OK. Let's go."

The hotel desk clerk drew out a little map to show us how to get to the drugstore, but we went a few blocks and realized we didn't know where we were or where we were going. In other words, we were lost. So we turned the dome light on and stopped the car to look at the hand-drawn map again. Just then a man's face appeared right at my door, pressed up against the window! He was wearing a ski cap pulled low over his head, and he just about scared me right into eternity. I yelled, "Liz, let's go! Just pull away. Go! Let's get out of here!"

We finally got to the drugstore and picked up the prescriptions. And on the way back, I said, "Now, Doug said to get some ripe bananas. But there's nothing open; everything's closed." Then, down the road, we saw a big, bright sign with just one four-letter word on it: "F-O-O-D." That's all it said, "FOOD," as though God were trying to keep things simple for us.

We pulled into the parking lot, and I told Liz, "Honey, you park by the door. You're young and cute, and I'm old and fat, so no one will bother me. Keep the motor running, keep the lights on, and lock the doors." (I don't have much faith. I've got a lot of joy, but you can't have every gift.) I told Liz to "stay right here by the door so nobody can get in or out. And if I'm not out in five minutes, you honk that horn and get the police."

So I went in, and right in front of me was a huge table filled with beautiful, yellow, ripe bananas! I couldn't believe it! That was the biggest miracle of all. So I shoved seven or eight bananas in a sack, paid the guy, jumped back in the car, and we were on our way back to deliver our emergency supplies to Mary.

The next morning Doug called and said, "I was just wondering how your big-shot friend is doing."

"Oh, she's doing fine!" I told him. "She's moving around and handling the whole thing just fine. Thanks so much, Doug. You *were* a ministering angel to all of us."

He paused a moment and said, "Barbara, I've been thinking. You know what I'd like to do, if you could help me? I'd like to start a ministry for people like you—for missionaries and Christian speakers who are on the road and get a sore throat or leg cramps. They could call a number and get a Christian doctor who could help them—give them suggestions and call in a prescription to wherever."

"Oh, Doug, that would be wonderful!" I exclaimed.

And the ripples in the pond just keep spreading outward . . .

## A Blessing Phenomenon

There's another phenomenon that happens when we pass on a blessing to someone else. It may defy the laws of physics; I don't know. But I'm convinced it happens. While a blessing of kindness ripples outward to others, it boomerangs right back to the one who threw the pebble. As one brokenhearted mother wrote in a letter to me, "God will take care of me, and I will do for others while God does for me. A great way to beat the blues is to do something for someone else." And another Christian wrote, "Those of us who have been saved should always be prepared to throw others a rope."

This isn't just the view of believers; it's been proved by scientific research. One report said recently that research had found that "doing for others . . . infuses people with vitality, purpose, happiness and health to heretofore unrecognized degrees."[3] It was a lesson illustrated by the loving actions of an eighty-eight-year-old mother who, every Sunday, pushed her fifty-year-old disabled son's wheelchair down the center aisle of a church to the front row where they sat so they could both hear. Every week an usher or friend offered to push the son's wheelchair for the old woman, and every week she politely declined the help. "No, thank you," she would say. "You see, I hold on to Michael's chair to keep *myself* from falling."

To paraphrase Proverbs 11:25, as we help others, we ourselves are helped.

**She who waters others will also be watered herself.**
**(Prov. 11:25 adapted)**

There are so many ways we can follow Jesus' example and be a servant to others. Sometimes we provide a gift of encouragement simply by doing ordinary work with cheerfulness. A friend's letter reminded me of that fact. She wrote to tell me about the death of her uncle.

He was a Christian. Hadn't had any serious illness. He and his wife . . . went to a Hardee's drive-through, and he ordered their breakfast. They ate there often, and the boy who took their order recognized my uncle's voice. The boy said, "Come on up, partner, we are waiting for you." Just then, my uncle grabbed his chest and said to his wife, "I'll see you in heaven!" And he was gone.

My aunt guided the car to a stop, and the boys at the counter came running out to help, but he was already gone . . .

At my uncle's funeral the minister said, "The voice over the speaker may have been the order-taker's, but it was a message straight from Jesus: 'Come on up, partner; we're waiting for you.'"

Isn't that sweet? So, it has been a great comfort to us to know our beloved uncle was welcomed home by Jesus—*over the speaker at Hardee's!*

If you thought your words would be the last earthly thing someone heard, would it make a difference in what you said or how you said it? In today's troubled world it's easy to be a pessimist. Anyone can spread that kind of message of gloom—"like clouds and wind without rain," as Proverbs 25:14 says. Instead, Christians need to be like the clouds that bring showers of blessings and encouragement to those who are struggling through a desert of despair.

## The Best Gift of All

When we're thinking of ways we can follow Jesus' example and show a servant's heart to those in need, there's no better gift we can give them than the hope of heaven! Many times, the only lifeline I've had to hang on to when I've landed in one of life's cesspools is the assurance that "this too shall pass"! We're only pilgrims here, not settlers, and the heavenly home we're promised will have no pain, no misery—nothing but joy! Hallelujah! As one friend said, "If we knew what God knows about heaven, we would clap our hands when a Christian dies."

The best illustration of the future that we Christians are promised is the following story by an unknown writer:

There was a woman who had been diagnosed with a terminal illness and had been given three months to live. So, as she was getting her things in order, she contacted

**THE FAMILY CIRCUS.**          **By Bil Keane**

© BKI

Reprinted with permission of Bil Keane.

"Grandma's right. There ARE lots of
people dying to get to heaven."

her pastor and had him come to her house to discuss certain aspects of her final wishes.

She told him which songs she wanted sung at the service, which Scriptures she would like read, and which outfit she wanted to be buried in. The woman also requested to be buried with her favorite Bible. Everything was in order, and the pastor was preparing to leave when the woman suddenly remembered something very important to her.

"There's one more thing," she said excitedly.

"What's that?" came the pastor's reply.

"This is very important," the woman continued. "I want to be buried with a fork in my right hand."

The pastor stood looking at the woman, not quite knowing what to say.

"That surprises you, doesn't it?" the woman asked.

"Well, to tell you the truth, I *am* puzzled by the request," said the pastor.

The woman explained, "In all my years of attending church socials and potluck dinners, I always remember that when the main course was being cleared away, someone would inevitably lean over and say, 'Keep your fork.' It was my favorite part because I knew that something better was coming . . . like velvety chocolate cake or lemon meringue pie. Something wonderful was coming, something with substance! So I just want people to see me there in that casket with a fork in my hand, and I want them to wonder, 'What's with the fork?' Then, I want you to tell them: 'Keep your fork. The best is yet to come.'"

The pastor's eyes welled up with tears of joy as he hugged the woman and said good-bye. He knew this was one of the last times he would see her. He also knew that this parishioner had a clear and insightful vision of heaven. She *knew* that something better was coming.

At the funeral, people were walking by the woman's casket and they saw the pretty dress she was wearing and her favorite Bible. That made sense. Then they saw the fork in her right hand. Over and over the pastor heard the question, "What's with the fork?" and over and over he smiled.

During his message, the pastor told the people of the conversation with the woman shortly before she died. He told them the fork story and what it meant to her.

*So the next time you reach down for your fork, let it remind you, oh, so gently, that* **the best is yet to come!**

The wonderful "fork story" always reminds me of another favorite line, one a friend included in a recent letter. She said, "Barb, after reading about some of your funny ways of looking at death, I came up with one of my own for my epitaph."

It's the perfect parting gift all Christians could give their loved ones, a reminder that we're enjoying the "dessert" of eternity:

> Don't cry for me.
> I'm finally where I want to be.

This dear woman has an eagerness for heaven that I share. The only thing different is that I may not have a tombstone to engrave. Bill and I want to donate our bodies to the local university—if they'll have us!

**Rubes**

**"I always thought that one day I'd donate my body to science, but I was kind of hoping it would be after I was dead."**

Billy Graham has also made it clear that he's enthusiastically looking forward to spending eternity in heaven. The last words in the book *Billy Graham: God's Ambassador* convey this enthusiasm in a most dramatic way. In script across the inside back cover of the book are these words:

> Someday you will read or hear that Billy Graham is dead. Don't you believe a word of it! I shall be more alive then than I am now. I will just have changed my address. I will have gone into the presence of God.[4]

A friend sent me a card last year that said, "When I was growing up in an East Texas farming community, we had an old-fashioned custom of 'walking a piece of the way home' with our visitors. Guests who walked to our house were accompanied halfway home after their visits. As a little girl, I welcomed this extra time I could spend with a cherished friend. Often these were the most delightful moments of all. I'm a good deal older now, and life's day is growing shorter. I am nevertheless comforted that I have walked at least part of the way home with a Friend—One who walks with me always, everywhere."

Now imagine the joy of passing along that blessing and walking someone else "halfway home" to heaven. Wouldn't it be marvelous to join that heavenly throng and have someone say, "Because of YOU, I accepted Jesus' invitation to spend eternity with Him"? It would be almost as wonderful as hearing the Savior say these words of gracious welcome:

Come, you who are blessed by my Father; take your inheritance, the kingdom prepared for you since the creation of the world.
    For I was hungry and you gave me something to eat,
I was thirsty and you gave me something to drink,
I was a stranger and you invited me in,
I needed clothes and you clothed me,
I was sick and you looked after me,
I was in prison and you came to visit me. . . .
Whatever you did for one of the least of these brothers of mine, you did for me.[5]

If I've managed to earn the gift of hearing those marvelous words someday, I can just imagine that my friend Sam Butcher's reminder will be ringing through my memory next, saying, *That's what it's all about, isn't it, Barb?*

# ACKNOWLEDGMENTS

If your heart has been touched or your day has been brightened by reading this book, credit is due to the many friends of Spatula Ministries who sent jokes, stories, poems, and zany insights to be shared with you for just this reason. We have made diligent effort to identify the original sources of this material, but sometimes this goal was impossible. Other times our research turned up multiple sources for the same item. Whenever the source of an unattributed item in this book can be positively identified, please contact Word Publishing, P.O. Box 141000, Nashville, TN 37214, so that proper credit can be given in future printings.

Grateful acknowledgment is also given for:

The mammogram essay on page 75 from *And How Are We Feeling Today?* by Kathryn Hammer © 1993. Used with permission of NTC/Contemporary Publishing Group.

The wonderful artwork and enduring patience of artist Dennis Hill.

The delightfully creative illustrations and story related to Colossians 3:12–14 by Marcey Hripak.

"If I Had My Child to Raise Over Again" by Diane Loomans. From the book *Full Esteem Ahead* © 1994 by Diane Loomans with Julia Loomans. Reprinted by permission of H. J. Kramer, P.O. Box 1082, Tiburon, CA. All rights reserved.

Endearing stories and incidents shared by Evelyn Maxey, Julie Hendry, Elizabeth Dent, and Sarah Rawley.

"Top Ten Reasons Why Heaven's Looking Good" by Fred Sanford. Used by permission.

"Parallels between writing a novel and having a baby," by Ed Stewart, writing for Tyndale House Publishers' "Page Turner's Journal," in Spring 1999, which I adapted for chapter 1.

# NOTES

**Chapter 1: Having a Baby Is Like Writing a Book—Lots of Whining, Begging, and Pushing**

1. The idea for this comparison came from Ed Stewart's essay, "An Author Speaks: Ed Stewart describes some parallels between writing a novel and having a baby," which appeared in "The Page Turner's Journal," an editorial/advertising newsletter by Tyndale House Publishers included in *Marriage Partnership*, spring 1999, and in *Today's Christian Woman*, March/April 1999. Used by permission.

2. "*CBA Marketplace's* Top 10 Best-Selling Nonfiction Books of 1997," *CBA Marketplace*, February 1998, 12. *Estrogen* was still making appearances on the bestseller list in 1999 while I was working on this book.

3. Dave Meurer, *Boyhood Daze: An Incomplete Guide to Raising Boys* (Minneapolis: Bethany House, 1999), 17–18.

4. Adapted from "Gladly," Faith & Values Section, *Minneapolis Star Tribune*.

**Chapter 2: Who Are These Kids, and Why Are They Calling Me Mom?**

1. Dru Sefton, "The Wonderful and the Wacky: Here's a mother-lode of moms who keep their kids in stitches," *Kansas City Star*, 9 May 1999, G1–2.

2. Linda Davenport, "Dancing with Mom," *Kansas City Star Magazine*, 9 May 1999, 13.

3. Original source unknown. Adapted from Alice Gray, *Stories for a Woman's Heart* (Sisters, Oreg.: Multnomah: 1999), 63.

4. Meryl Streep, quoted in Steve Persall, "Mother of Invention," *Tampa Tribune*, 18 September 1999, D-1.

5. Robert Lee Hotz, "Pregnancy may increase brain power," *Los Angeles Times*, reprinted in the *Tampa Tribune*, 11 December 1998.

6. Caryle Murphy, "Motorists see signs from 'God,'" *Washington Post*, reprinted in the *Denver Post*, 9 July 1999, 1.

7. Diane Loomans, "If I Had My Child to Raise Over Again," *Full Esteem Ahead: 100 Ways to Build Self-Esteem in Children and Adults* (Triburon, Calif.: H. J. Kramer, 1994). Used by permission.

8. Mike Atkinson, Mikey's Funnies, Youth Ministry on the Net: http://www.Youthspecialties.com.

9. Meurer, *Boyhood Daze*, 13.

10. Mary Jo Malone, "Of love and leave-taking: Does it ever get easy?" *St. Petersburg Times*, 6 April 1999, B1.

11. Barb Greco, in a letter to Oprah Winfrey on *The Oprah Winfrey Show*, 14 July 1999.

## Chapter 3: How to Be a Joyful Woman—Take Up Acting

1. Associated Press writer Daniel Q. Haney, "Study: Mental stress can cause long-term damage to the heart," *The Register*, 10 March 1999, 7.

2. "My brethren, count it all joy when ye fall into divers temptations; knowing this, that the trying of your faith worketh patience" (James 1:2–3 KJV).

3. Psalm 145:14 TLB.

4. Habakkuk 3:17–19.

5. Suzanne Farnham, founder of the Listening Hearts ministry in Baltimore, quoted in Ed Stannard, "The Spirit speaks to us, if we can learn to listen," *Episcopal Life*, February 1999, 16.

6. Norman Vincent Peale, *Enthusiasm Makes the Difference*. This excerpt, along with the discussion of "act as if," is adapted from Rob Gilbert, Ph.D., "The Three Most Powerful Words in the English Language," a *Bits & Pieces* booklet published by The Economics Press, 12 Daniel Road, Fairfield, NJ 07004-2565.

7. Charles H. Gabriel, "Brighten the Corner Where You Are," 1913.

8. George F. Will, "Pithy words of wisdom to Class of '99," *Tampa Tribune*, 10 June 1999, A15.

9. William James, quoted in Gilbert, "The Three Most Powerful Words in the English Language," 5.

10. Source unknown.

11. David Flick, "Don't Worry About Being Happy," *Dallas Morning News*, July 1999.

12. *Bits & Pieces*, 15 July 1999, 7.

13. Ibid., 23.

### Chapter 4: I Finally Got My Head Together—Then My Body Fell Apart!

1. Sam Levenson, *In One Era and Out the Other* (New York: Simon and Schuster, 1973), 176–77.

2. Doreen Iudica Vigue, "Americans' appetite grows for all things gargantuan," Boston Globe, reprinted in *Memphis Commercial Appeal*, 18 April 1999, A18.

3. Ellen Goodman, "Americans grow into their food in giant economy-size portions," *Boston Globe*, published in the *Tampa Tribune*, 3 March 1999, 15.

4. "For some Nigerians, womanhood begins in 'fattening room,'" *Los Angeles Times*, published in *St. Petersburg Times*, 16 October 1998, 21A.

5. Kathryn Hammer, *And How Are We Feeling Today?* (Chicago: Contemporary Books, 1993), 72–73. Used by permission.

6. Colossians 3:12–14 NKJV.

7. Thanks to Darcey Hripak, Port Washington, New York, for sharing this delightful story and the accompanying illustrations.

8. Adapted from Peggy Ryan, quoted in Roz Warren, ed., *Women's Lip* (Napierville, Ill.: Sourcebooks, 1999), 24.

### Chapter 5: We Started Out with Nothing—and Still Have Most of It Left

1. Jane Clapperton, "Finders Weepers," *Woman's Day*, 2 October 1984, 138.

2. "Don't leave the market without it," *St. Petersburg Times*, 7 August 1999, Home and Garden section, 1.

3. "Strangers in Strange Lands," *Arkansas Democrat Gazette*, 10 January 1999, H1.

4. "Objects of Desire: Sink Job," *Denver Post,* 5 June 1999, Scene section, 1.

5. Dave Gussow, "High tech @ home," *St. Petersburg Times,* 21 June 1999, Tech Times section, 11.

6. Judy Stark, ed., "No-dish Dessert," *Tampa Tribune,* Homes 1, 22 May 1999.

7. Mary Hunt, "Tiptionary," *Cheapskate Monthly,* February 1999, 7.

8. *Bits & Pieces,* 6 November 1997, 15.

9. 1 Corinthians 13:1–8, *The Message,* with added paraphrase.

10. Tal D. Bonham and Jack Gulledge, *The Treasury of Clean Senior Adult Jokes* (Nashville: Broadman, 1989), 121.

11. Ibid., 103.

12. Ibid., 18.

13. Doc Blakely, "Laughter, the Best Medicine," *Reader's Digest,* August 1999, 89.

14. Adapted from Phyllis Diller, quoted in Warren, *Women's Lip,* 53.

**Chapter 6: If They Can Send a Man to the Moon . . . Why Can't They Send 'Em All?**

1. George F. Will, "The Perils of Brushing," citing a report by *American Enterprize* magazine in *Newsweek,* 10 May 1999, 92.

2. Psychologist David Lewis, cited in "Loose Change: Shopping. It's War," *St. Petersburg Times,* 17 January 1999, Money & Business section, 1.

3. Tom Zucco, "Wild & Wooly," *St. Petersburg Times,* 19 February 1999, Floridian section, 1.

4. Laura Bush, quoted in *Redbook,* August 1999.

5. Jeffery Sobal, Cornell University, quoted by Natalie Angier, New York Times Syndicate, reprinted in "Marriage maxim adjusted," *Denver Post,* 8 July 1998, 3F.

6. Maradee A. Davis, University of California at San Francisco, cited by Angier, "Marriage maxim adjusted," ibid.

7. David Broder, *Washington Post* Writers Group, "An unmatched American life," *St. Petersburg Times,* 21 March 1999, 7A.

8. Charis Collins, "Serendipitous but eternal enmeshment," *Oregonian,* First Person Singular, 14 February 1999, L3.

9. Adapted from *Episcopal Life,* March 1999, 2.

## Chapter 7: When Your Road Is All Downhill, You're Probably Holding the Map Upside Down

1. Betty Boyd Eigenauer, "Good Times Await Seniors," letters to the editor, *Orange County Register,* undated clipping.

2. Associated Press, "Study finds similarities among people who live past 100," *Tampa Tribune,* 20 April 1999, 8A.

3. Stephaan Harris, "Most reject the growing opportunity to live to 100," *USA Today,* 26 May 1999, D1.

4. Knight Ridder Newspapers, "More Americans reaching 100, and they're healthier," *St. Petersburg Times,* 18 August 1999, 4A.

5. Associated Press, "98-year-old dance student doesn't miss a single beat," *Tampa Tribune,* 31 August 1998.

6. Rick Folstad, "A Class by Herself," *Denver Rocky Mountain News,* 30 May 1999, 40R.

7. Anne Dingus, "Small Town Heroes," *Texas Monthly,* March 1999, 144.

8. Associated Press, "At 108, woman recalls momentous, mundane," *St. Petersburg Times,* 26 April 1999, 5B.

9. Eric Deggans, "Tale of two remarkable sisters," *St. Petersburg Times,* 18 April 1999, 8F.

10. Advertisement, "At 101 years old, Leila Denmark, M.D., is the oldest practicing physician in the U.S.," *Wall Street Journal,* 15 September 1999, B5.

11. Associated Press, "Study: Women find menopause a fulfilling stage," *St. Petersburg Times,* 5 September 1997, 4A.

12. "The Estrogen Fairy Tale," a product of DonEl, Pittsburgh, Penna.

13. Dave Barry, *Dave Barry Turns 50* (New York: Crown, 1998), quoted in Dave Barry, "Can You See Turning 50? Or, Turning 50, Can You See?" *Dallas Morning News,* 27 September 1998, F1, 7.

14. Max Lucado, *A Gentle Thunder* (Nashville: Word, 1995), 60.

15. Michael Precker, "At What Year Should Those Birthday Messages Turn Kinder and Gentler?" *Dallas Morning News,* 27 September 1998, F1, 9.

16. This item appeared in the Ann Landers column, Creators Syndicate, 14 May 1999.

17. "LifeWatch" column, *Philadelphia Inquirer,* 3 October 1999.

18. Craig Wilson, "The good old days, we hardly knew you," *USA Today*, 3–6 September 1999, 1.

19. Sue Landry, "A whole new world, in a sense," *St. Petersburg Times*, 18 April 1999, F1.

20. Steve Martin, *Pure Drivel* (New York: Hyperion, 1998), quoted in Curt Schleier, "Two wild and crazy guys," *St. Petersburg Times*, 27 September 1998, 6D.

21. "Laughter, the Best Medicine," *Reader's Digest*, August 1999, 88.

**Chapter 8: Sliding Down a Rainbow, into a Pool of Joy!**

1. Adapted from Larrene Hagaman's column "From the Chapel," in *Chapel Bells* magazine, Vicki Cash, editor, Fall 1999, 6–7. Published by Precious Moments, P. O. Box 802, Carthage, MO 64836.

2. Mark 1:41.

3. "Successful Aging: A Lifestyle Choice," a report on the MacArthur Foundation Study of Aging in America, *St. Louis Times*, August 1998, 7.

4. *Billy Graham: God's Ambassador* (New York: Time-Life, 1999).

5. Matthew 25:34–36, 40.

### Mama Get The Hammer! There's A Fly On Papa's Head
0-8499-3417-6 ◆ Trade Paper ◆ $10.99
0-8499-6192-0 ◆ Audio ◆ $10.99
Barbara Johnson insists that laughing in the face of adversity is not a form of denial, but a proven tool for managing stress, coping with pain, and maintaining hope. She zeroes directly in on the spiritual benefit of a smile, a giggle, and a good, old-fashioned belly laugh.

### Pack Up Your Gloomees in a Great Big Box, Then Sit On The Lid and Laugh
0-8499-3364-1 ◆ Trade Paper ◆ $10.99
0-8499-6077-0 ◆ Audio ◆ $10.99
*Pack Up Your Gloomees* is filled with bittersweet stories of Barbara's journey through the minefields of life, and her wise and encouraging responses to letters from hurting parents. Each chapter ends with a laughter-packed Gloomee Buster.

### Splashes of Joy in the Cesspools of Life
0-8499-3313-7 ◆ Trade Paper ◆ $10.99
0-8499-6051-7 ◆ Audio ◆ $10.99
0-8499-3941-0 ◆ Large Print ◆ $14.99
Barbara Johnson's approach to life is positive, uplifting, and fun. *Splashes of Joy* offers an invigorating spurt of encouragement and a gentle reminder to splash joy into the lives of others.

### Stick A Geranium in Your Hat and Be Happy!

0-8499-3201-7 ◆ Trade Paper ◆ $10.99
0-8499-1260-1 ◆ Audio ◆ $10.99
0-8499-3683-7 ◆ Large Print ◆ $14.99

This is the book that started it all! A survivor of four devastating experiences that equip her with the credentials to help others work through their own pain, Barbara Johnson discovers hope in the hurt and shows while pain is inevitable, misery is optional.

## Now Kids and Grandkids Can Experience the Geranium Lady

*How do you explain concepts like God's love or true joy to kids? In Barbara Johnson's fun new children's series, kids will laugh as they learn about these truths through the Geranium Lady's zany adventures.*

### The Upside-Down Frown and Splashes of Joy

0-8499-5844-X ◆ Hard Cover ◆ $7.99

The Geranium Lady and her young friend learn the real secret to turning frowns upside down into smiles. Includes a special Make Your Own "Splashes of Joy!" section.

### Super-Scrumptious Jelly Donuts Sprinkled with Hugs

0-8499-5848-2 ◆ Hard Cover ◆ $7.99

In this book, the Geranium Lady introduces kids to hugs through a contest. After much laughter and fun, everyone learns that God invented hugs as a way for people to show they care. Includes simple instructions for children to make their very own HUG coupons.

*This book has been enjoyed by
and shared with:*

_____

_____

_____

_____

_____

_____

_____

_____

_____

_____

_____

_____

_____